Praise for *Whole Life Transformation*

"Many people struggle to know how to 'do church' in light of spiritual formation. Finally, here is the book they've been looking for."

Jan Johnson, spiritual director and author of *Invitation to the Jesus Life*

"Thank you, Keith, for writing authentically and lovingly about the need for churches, ministries and believers to bridge the transformation gap from a halfway gospel into the abundant life of Christ's kingdom."

Stephen A. Macchia, president, Leadership Transformations, and author of *Becoming a Healthy Church*

"Keith Meyer reminds us that Christian discipleship requires a whole life transformation which converts the heart, its values and its relationships so that the world can be transformed. This book is unnerving and unsettling—in the gospel sense!"

Albert Haase, O.F.M., author of *Coming Home to Your True Self* and *Living the Lord's Prayer*

"I know you can't see me, but I am giving Keith Meyer a standing ovation. . . . I love Keith's joy, honesty, energy and his overactive mind. . . . He has got the gospel right, the church right and life right. . . . He also has being with God right."

Bill Hull, author of *Christlike: The Pursuit of Uncomplicated Obedience*

"In *Whole Life Transformation* Meyer shines a bright and grace-filled light on the problem [with the spirituality of church]. His insights are crystal clear. Best of all, . . . he supplies doable practices toward all of us becoming the change our churches need."

Todd Hunter, Anglican bishop and author of *Giving Church Another Chance*

"In this fine book, Keith Meyer draws on the deep wells of the church fathers as well as the wisdom of Dallas Willard to offer us a drink of water in the midst of the desert that pastoral ministry has become. As a fine thinker, a student of theology and a pastor, Meyer offers us a clear, practical pathway out because he himself has walked it."

David Fitch, professor of evangelical theology, Northern Baptist Theological Seminary

"Keith Meyer is the type of person you want to spend time with. He is transparent, well read, fun-loving, irreverent and deeply spiritual. . . . *Whole Life Transformation* is a perfect reflection of the author, and it's a book about spiritual transformation written by an experienced pastor who has lived the journey. It's his first book, but it sure won't be his last."

Gary W. Moon, vice president, Richmont Graduate University, and author of *Apprenticeship with Jesus*

"With refreshing candor and honest confession Keith Meyer takes us on a wonderful journey that will pull you in and knock you out (in a good way!) with its potent critique of our modern church compulsions, activities and teachings that dominate church life, yet constantly leave us longing for true and lasting change. . . . I heartily commend [this book] to all Christian leaders who want to lead a new kind of church."

Keith J. Matthews, professor, Azusa Pacific University Graduate School

"Get to know Keith Meyer and the Jesus he knows. You will become the change your church, your family and your world need—whole life transformation!"

Howard Baker, instructor of Christian formation, Denver Seminary, and author of *The One True Thing*

"On some level every pastor will identify with Meyer's dysfunctional experience in ministry. He asks why so many of us fail to experience the transforming power of Christ we proclaim. That is a dangerous question, but Meyer's raw honesty is matched with a hope-filled rediscovery of the gospel."

Skye Jethani, author of *The Divine Commodity* and managing editor of *Leadership Journal*

"Keith Meyer's *Whole Life Transformation* is a compelling invitation. His particular blend of divine grace, community life, intentional discipline, inner healing and a sense of humor is a blue-ribbon recipe for Christian maturity. . . . We cannot read this book and rest satisfied in a complacent Christian walk."

Evan B. Howard, director of Spirituality Shoppe: An Evangelical Center for the Study of Christian Spirituality

"Keith Meyer encourages and challenges us to reach far beyond the quantity of disciples to where the impact lies—quality of disciples. . . . I was challenged on a personal level and inspired on a leadership level as I read. For anyone interested in measuring quality, this is a must-read book."

Don Cousins, speaker, consultant and author of *Experiencing LeaderShift*

"This is a prophetic book that is not angry, for the author more often points the finger at himself than at anyone else. Not content to simply describe his own wanderings, he graciously and concretely invites Christian leaders to follow Jesus more closely and receive his wisdom and healing."

James C. Wilhoit, Scripture Press Professor of Christian Formation and Ministry, Wheaton College

"If you're a Christian leader longing for something more, then *Whole Life Transformation* may be your open door for personal and ministry renewal. . . . Keith's story offers Christian leaders some practical ways to engage in their own personal journey that can lead to churchwide whole life transformation."

Klaus Issler, author of *Wasting Time with God*

"This is an immensely honest and practical book—a desperately needed book. . . . The author challenges 'the reduced gospel' in order to call all who know Jesus to the work of the Holy Spirit in transforming our lives privately, relationally, communally, publicly and in ministry."

Richard E. Averbeck, professor of Old Testament and Semitic languages, Trinity Evangelical Divinity School

Whole Life Transformation

BECOMING THE CHANGE YOUR CHURCH NEEDS

KEITH MEYER

FOREWORD BY DALLAS WILLARD

IVP Books

An imprint of InterVarsity Press
Downers Grove, Illinois

InterVarsity Press
P.O. Box 1400, Downers Grove, IL 60515-1426
World Wide Web: www.ivpress.com
E-mail: email@ivpress.com

InterVarsity Press® is the book-publishing division of InterVarsity Christian Fellowship/USA®, a
movement of students and faculty active on campus at hundreds of universities, colleges and
schools of nursing in the United States of America, and a member movement of the International
Fellowship of Evangelical Students. For information about local and regional activities, write
Public Relations Dept., InterVarsity Christian Fellowship/USA, 6400 Schroeder Rd., P.O. Box
7895, Madison, WI 53707-7895, or visit the IVCF website at <www.intervarsity.org>.

All Scripture quotations, unless otherwise indicated, are taken from the Holy Bible, New
International Version®. NIV®. Copyright ©1973, 1978, 1984 by International Bible Society.
Used by permission of Zondervan Publishing House. All rights reserved.

Design: Cindy Kiple

Images: man on a ladder looking at sky: Kamil Vojnar/Getty Images
        yosemite church: jason woodcock/iStockphoto

ISBN 978-0-8308-3530-0

Printed in the United States of America ∞

Library of Congress Cataloging-in-Publication Data

Meyer, Keith, 1955-
  Whole life transformation: becoming the change your church needs /
Keith Meyer.
       p. cm.
  Includes bibliographical references.
  ISBN 978-0-8308-3530-0 (hardcover: alk. paper)
  1. Clergy—Religious life. 2. Spiritual formation. I. Title.
  BV4011.6.M49 2010
  248.8'92—dc22

                                                                    2010008333

| P | 18 | 17 | 16 | 15 | 14 | 13 | 12 | 11 | 10 | 9 | 8 | 7 | 6 | 5 | 4 | 3 | 2 | 1 |
| Y | 25 | 24 | 23 | 22 | 21 | 20 | 19 | 18 | 17 | 16 | 15 | 14 | 13 | 12 | 11 | 10 |

To my "formation family"
best friend and soulmate, Cheri,
adult children and friends, Kyle, Cara and Mike . . .
Your pursuit of a kingdom life
has made you containers of God's blessings to me.
You graciously keep on calling me "home"
to know a good life with you and our good God

In a well-furnished kitchen there are not only crystal goblets and silver platters, but waste cans and compost buckets—some containers used to serve fine meals, others to take out the garbage. Become the kind of container God can use to present any and every kind of gift to his guests for their blessing.

2 TIMOTHY 2:20-21 THE MESSAGE

Ascend my brothers, ascend eagerly. . . . Run I beg you, run with him who said, "Let us hurry until we all arrive at the unity of faith and of the knowledge of God . . . mature . . . at the measure of the stature of Christ's fullness."

JOHN CLIMACUS, THE LADDER OF DIVINE ASCENT

And in the end, what God gets out of your ministry . . . is you.

DALLAS WILLARD

Contents

Foreword

W*hole Life Transformation* places before us exactly what its title suggests. The message is that success in ministry and in life is found by becoming *on the "inside"* the kind of person who lives in the kingdom of God here and now. This person is led by their confidence in Jesus to *seek* the kingdom of God, to seek to live in it, more than anything else and in all places. As they do this, transformation into Christlikeness progresses, and they find that, more and more, they easily and routinely do the kinds of things practiced and taught by Jesus Christ. Spiritual formation in Christ is the process that occurs to those who have, by grace and by choice, entered into the status of the disciple or apprentice of Jesus in kingdom living.

Two things currently tend to defeat discipleship and transformation among Christians. First is the theology—the soteriology—that being a Christian has nothing essentially to do with being a disciple. Being a disciple is an add-on, an option, which the Christian is free to choose or omit. Salvation is forgiveness and that is secured by accepting a particular theory of the atonement. Salvation therefore has nothing to do with discipleship or transformation, nor they with it. James B. Torrance and many others have pointed out that this omits living in the trinitarian community. It omits taking on the nature of the Father and dwelling in the goodness and righteousness of his family. This in turn redefines the gospel and makes success in "church work" a matter of getting as many people as possible (supposedly) ready to die. That becomes a matter of technique, and leadership a matter for experts in the technique. The soul of the leader withers, and often, they think, it is all "for the sake of the work."

The second obstructive idea derives from the first. It is the idea that discipleship to Jesus is something religious, that it is "church work." It has to do only with religious activities as defined by religious activities. So it is thought. But because discipleship is a matter of learning to live, discipleship is a matter of our whole life. Its primary place is where we live: our home and our work. Discipleship is for the world, in the sense of ordinary life—*whole life*—and it only occurs in that world. Church activity, if it is to be successful in God's terms, is in support of such discipleship. The church is for discipleship, and discipleship is for the world as God's place. This is what the "Great Commission" of Matthew 28 plainly says. (See also Col 3:17.)

What all of this means in practice is that *relationships* form the receptacle for receiving the fullness of Christ and are the place where the kingdom comes and God's will is to be done as it is "in the heavens." Church relationships, too, and that would be a great step forward. But *all* relationships: first to God, then to everyone with whom I am in meaningful contact, my "neighbors." This has to be done from the inside, where love, joy, peace, patience, kindness, generosity, faithfulness, gentleness and self-control come to reign supreme and in unison over all that is done. We grow into this, "learn" it, as students or apprentices to Christ. The idea that there is something else that can take the place of this, or that this can be omitted in favor of "service," is a primary delusion of Satan over the world order—and often over the "church" order.

Keith Meyer has suffered the consequences of these two theological barriers to whole life transformation in both his personal journey and in his service as a minister. But he has now come to insightful and biblical terms with them and can help us move beyond them to understandings and practices of kingdom living that will lift us into trinitarian fellowship and obedience to Christ from transformed "insides." *Whole Life Transformation* therefore is not just another analysis of what's wrong but, more importantly, is a trustworthy guide to what is right: one drawn both from the author's own experience and from the Bible and the wisdom of Christ, proven in the experience of his people throughout the ages.

This is a hopeful book that brings helpful solutions, pointing the way to the life that God upholds and blesses, and giving directions for entering that life and growing there. In this way it also shows how such a life can rule and guide Christian groups through authentic discipleship to Jesus, the King and the Master. It is written out of much pain and deep learnings that have drawn the author off the beaten path of contemporary evangelicalism and guided him into the way of companionship with Jesus 24/7. In so doing it revives the age-old heart of evangelicalism.

Now is our time. By far the most powerful "church-growth plan" ever implemented is that of the Great Commission. Its incredible effect on the world in the times immediately following its impartation was due to the *whole life transformation* it brought to millions of ordinary people who, as disciples, were taught to do and lead others to do "all things, whatsoever I have commanded you." Have you got a better idea?

Dallas Willard

Introduction

Dad, Are You Home Yet?

One day I came home early. I had piles of work on my desk in the church office but had promised myself and my wife, Cheri, I would spend some "quality time" with my six-year-old son, Kyle. Quality time for Kyle sometimes meant watching cartoons with him, and today that was just what I needed; some vegetative TV watching. I plopped myself next to him on the couch, joining him in his cartoon reverie.

And then I noticed that I was really tired. But not just physically; I was tired of ministry and the kind of life it seemed to require of me. I was preaching, teaching and creating programs about living the Christian life and getting to heaven, but I was living in what seemed like a kind of hell on earth.

I had grown up a pastor's kid, and time spent at church or in ministry activities often edged out time at home. I was now modeling to my family what I had been shown as the right way to serve the church and God. Consequently, Cheri and I were having arguments about how I was spending my time. Too many nights out each week, long hours and preoccupation with ministry were not what she had signed up for when saying "I do." Looking back on it now I can see that I was pursuing a twisted idea of success, not in the secular forms I regularly preached against but in the sanctified activism and workaholism often seen in professional ministry. A growing church, defined mostly by higher attendance at church services, more and more programs, and bigger budgets and buildings, was the marks of a successful ministry in the clergy circles I ran with. I was not alone in this pursuit or the harried kind of life it seemed to require.

More often than not, at denominational conferences the conversation would soon turn to church attendance figures or building programs. A subtle form of ambition seemed just below the surface of our desire to grow our ministries. Although uneasy with the practice, I often found myself comparing my age and the size of my congregation with my father's at the same age. At thirty my father had one thousand at worship. I had five hundred. I lose—both at ministry and family.

So on that day while vegging out with little Kyle at my side, a jolting question broke the drone of the TV.

Without even looking at me he asked, "Dad, are you home yet?"

His question hit me as strange and surprising. Home yet? What did he mean? Hadn't I been sitting there with him for at least twenty minutes, watching his favorite cartoon?

I didn't quite know how to answer his question. It reminded me of my wife's complaints of how absent or distant I had been to her. His question shined a searchlight on what I had excused as my spiritual duty. The life I was living had become deformed and driven. I was standing at the center of an orbit that was spinning out of control and about to split in a million directions, fueled by just as many good intentions.

A GAPING HOLE
Kyle's question had awakened me to some gaping holes in the

fabric of my life. At the center was the hole in my heart that I had thought ministry would fill. I did not have a fulfilling life with God but needed to act like I had one. And then there was the hole in my social life. Besides the distance between Cheri, Kyle and me, we didn't have the kind of friendships in or outside of the church we could trust. There was the hole in my character. I was filled with worry, lust, anger, contempt and ambition, and a sense of the hypocrisy of preaching and teaching how-to sermons on living for Jesus that weren't working in my own life. I had claimed and reclaimed forgiveness for these issues, but I wasn't experiencing any release or growth. So, I began to measure the distance between who I was and who I wanted to be, between what ministry was and what it should be, and prayed that somehow God would fill in the holes and close the gaps.

But was any other kind of life possible? Was there another way to live? Was there a way home to the life I sometimes caught a glimpse of in Scripture but didn't think possible in real life? And if so, where would I find it?

About this time a friend suggested I read Dallas Willard's *Spirit of the Disciplines*. The book helped me see things in the Bible in such a different light that I began to hope for a different kind of life. I read that life in Christ was more than just being forgiven of sin; it was having power over sin and a new kind of life, one rich in relationships. Christ's commandments, which call us to the reality of a life not ruled by anger, contempt, worry, lust and the isolation these produce, were meant to be obeyed so that we could live like Jesus and love others as he did. And freedom from these sinful attitudes and behaviors could actually become the atmosphere of our lives rather than occasional whiffs of an existence found only in the afterlife. Willard also claimed that the process of becoming like Jesus is not to be a "pose or by a constant and grinding effort, but with ease and power," which he called the "easy yoke" or way of Jesus.

Dallas Willard not only thought change was possible, he said it might even be easier on the soul and body than disobedience, or as Scripture puts it, Jesus' commands are not burdensome, and the life Jesus offers is a "winning" one that others will desire when they see it in us. This is what God actually intends and is planning on, the fact that *we* would become the change needed in our churches. We pastors and leaders are his program, "the program" he wanted for whole life transformation in his church.

It was hard to admit, but I didn't see obedience as more attractive than sin. And sinning sure seemed easier than obeying. How could not being angry be better? It worked so well in getting others to do what I wanted. And what would I do without worry? It was the way I motivated myself into getting things done.

Many of the pastors and congregants I knew were wrestling with the difficulty of trying to live what they read in their Bibles. Some, like me, waffled between either faking it, grinding it out, taking it for granted or giving up entirely—few if any appeared to live in such a way that others would want the kind of life they lived. And now my own life "for God" was distancing me from my family. I couldn't go back, I was ready for more.

I didn't start out with noble ideas of becoming some kind of a saint (my family and coworkers will assure you—I don't ever need to worry about that). I just wanted to have my family back. The process of putting *The Spirit of the Disciplines* into practice is my story of whole life transformation—a change in me that was needed first before I could partner with God for any kind of change in my church. It sparked my imagination. I now understood not only what a truly transformed person would look like but also how a marriage, friendships, a church, the body of Christ in a city, and eventually, in God's time, a whole world could be transformed.

So I set out on this journey while serving in my second church, where I was senior pastor. It entailed taking a painful but healing year away from ministry. After learning a new way to live I was led back into ministry to serve as executive pastor of the Church of the Open Door. While I am no longer at Open Door, it was the context for much the writing of this book. And I currently share this journey with students I teach at seminaries as well as with pastors at conferences, retreats and consultations.

Having tried and tested this new kind of life and having met others who have experienced the same, I have come to believe that God is calling the church to recover the life that is ours in Christ, a life that the Holy Spirit keeps on breathing into the church. I write as a Protestant evangelical who has found the life of Jesus alive and well in the broader church, both ancient and modern, from expressions such as Roman Catholicism and Quakerism of the West to that of the Egyptian desert communities and the Eastern Orthodox of the East. I hope my story will help you to find your way home, and you too will be able to share it with others. Kyle's question made me aware of how far I was from the life Christ offers, but even more questions were raised as I started to find my way home to transformation.

1

The Transformation Gap

How could I be so sure of being saved and on the way to my home in heaven when I was so far away from home in my present life? And how did the gap between the two develop in the first place?

My conversion to Christ had brought an initial spurt of change but soon settled down into basically the same old life when measured by my experience of anger, rage, worry, pride and self-centeredness. I wasn't partying hard, but neither were most of my non-Christian friends. What was the difference between them and me? Was it just that I was forgiven? I was leading people to Christ and doing many good things for people, but something was missing. While I preached on loving our enemies, I too often lived in contempt of anyone who got in the way of my ministry goals, and now that included my own wife!

This led me to a reexamination of what the Bible calls "the abundant life." I concluded that there was indeed a difference between the kind of life exemplified by Jesus and Paul, and which Jesus calls us to, and what my expectations were for life in Christ. In my ministry I became aware that most people don't believe the life exemplified by Jesus and Paul is possible today. At best it may have been possible for a few "star athletes," biblical heroes who no longer exist.

But to my surprise I found in my study of church history that deep and radical life change was not only possible but was expected of believers as recently as the late nineteenth century. The transformed life was seen as the church's main mission, and without it others wondered whether a person was saved or if the church was still on task. Somewhere after the Second Great Awakening (1790-1840s) the expectation of transformation was diminished. Among evangelicals the transmission of new life in Christ by example, imitation and training in a "living faith" was reduced to a weakened understanding of discipleship. Disciples of Jesus were no longer made, just converts who were Christian in name and doctrinal beliefs only.

THE TRANSFORMATION GAP APPEARS

Henry Ward Beecher, a great preacher and national leader of the late nineteenth century, exemplifies the shift in Christian expectations. He struggled with his marriage and was at least inappropriate with several women under his ministry. He caused a national scandal by having an affair with a business associate's wife. Much like the biblical King David, Beecher tried to cover it up and intentionally ruined the jealous husband's career, which tarnished Beecher's national work toward abolishing slavery.

Underneath his hypocrisy was a strong belief in the God of love, but not the God who loved him enough to deliver him from sin. Sometime before his affair he expressed the dilemma his theology created in regard to God and his sins, "I know that he will forgive them—but will he deliver me from them?" he asked. "It is not a want of faith in Christ for the past that I lack—but, O, that I might have a Christ who should assure me of rescue and purity in every period of my life to come!"

It is uncertain whether he really came clean and owned up to his sin. He ended up being ridiculed but blindly supported by his church during a civil trial that held the nation's attention. The preacher was acquitted due to a "he said, she said" morass of circumstantial evidence.

His pitiful cry captures the growing ambiguity today regarding what change is possible for the followers of Jesus in this life. This tortured example of the fall of a well-known and productive Christian figure is one that has been repeated many times since. Sadly such behavior is not as shocking now as it was then. We do not flinch when famous or not-so-famous pastors fall. Pastors were once respected and trusted more than all other professionals but now fall just behind politicians and dangerously close to lawyers in the polls. How did this change come about?

Historian and theologian Richard Lovelace has correctly identified a gap or hole in current evangelical theology and experience. He termed it the "sanctification gap." The gap falls between God's initial work of justification and his final work of glorification. Sanctification is the process of becoming progressively more like Christ by cooperating with God to become holy. In terms of Christian spiritual formation, it is the *life change* or transformation that occurs after conversion and before death. In church history, sanctification is the element missing for the last one to two hundred years, at least since the last of the great American revivals. It is a "caught" more than "taught" living faith and is the "spiritual capital" of the church. Lovelace makes the point that, historically, revivals or awakenings resulted in radical change of life for individuals and for the society they lived in.

THE GAP'S LOWERED EXPECTATIONS

Since the appearance of the sanctification or transformation gap, the American church has experienced many more figures like Henry Ward Beecher. And these figures mirror what the

average Christian now believes is possible for their own character development and growth in Christlikeness. Leaders like Billy
Graham, whose lives evidence integrity, now seem to be the ex-
ception rather than the rule for church leaders. And their life is
not viewed as the norm for the lives of ordinary believers.

At a conference on formation I recently attended, one speaker
shared his sadness and disappointment that his fellow speakers
were referring to "nominal evangelicals," those who didn't share
the heart and life of the gospel of Jesus but still claimed to be
born again. The expectation of the average Christian for the
sanctified life has been lowered. We are in need of leaders who
once again set the bar high and personally evidence whole life
transformation as normal and expected for all Christians. Until
the recent past, the church has had these kind of leaders, who
were the source for inspiration and revival.

At a time when the church was being domesticated by the
Roman Empire, Augustine of Hippo was delivered from sexual
promiscuity to pen a confession that has helped so many to set-
tle their restlessness in God's presence and love. And when the
medieval church was in ruins, Francis of Assisi, a notorious and
well-dressed disturber of the peace, took vows of poverty and
peacemaking, and single-handedly attempted to stop the Cru-
sades. And at a time when the church needed reformation, The-
resa of Ávila, a beautiful and self-centered young woman, turned
her body and soul into a castle ruled by God and was overcome
with the love of Christ for her. Through her writing many have
been introduced into that same intimate love.

Amazing Grace is the title of a Hollywood film about the life
of William Wilberforce, the English evangelical who led par-
liament in a thirty-year fight for the abolition of slavery in Brit-
ish Empire, which cost him his health and wealth. The self-
proclaimed former "wretch" and slaver trader, John Newton,

who wrote the hymn "Amazing Grace," is featured in this film, which recounts the changed lives of these men and their powerful influence on their world and culture.

The church also has a body of literature that recorded exemplary Christians' way of life for others to imitate. The fourteenth-century classic on formation titled *The Imitation of Christ*, by Thomas à Kempis, was instrumental in bringing John Newton to faith and to a radically new life in Christ. This book calls for transformation of life as the sign of genuine conversion and is second only to the Bible itself in Christian literature. It addresses tangible changes in behavior (e.g., forgiving our enemies and keeping the tongue from slander and gossip). It expects a change of life for those who know Christ and specifically calls into question those who can articulate theological concepts like the Trinity but show little evidence of trinitarian life and love. It is no wonder that it had an effect on Newton's conversion, leading to change in his character, occupation and worldview.

Today, leaders and books calling for and expecting significant change in believers are rare. Instead, we find award-ceremony testimonies of celebrity athletes or stars who thank God for their success, calling it his blessing. Some writers even suggest that significant progress in obedience in this life is not possible. There is a growing acceptance of the transformation gap being the normal Christian experience. Grace settles our eternal destiny, but we will have to wait until we get to heaven for it to do much more for us. Our life on earth becomes more of a waiting room than an adventure or journey with God.

Sadly, now even pastors and leaders no longer expect significant life change for Christians. The kind of life Jesus presents in the Sermon on the Mount—free of worry, lust, anger, contempt, gossip and greed—is not seen as possible. As the bumper sticker

says, "Christians aren't perfect, just forgiven." Progress in holiness is not expected in this life despite the many Scriptures that
admonish us to grow in grace. It seems that God's amazing
grace is not so amazing; it just offers us unconditional acceptance and freedom from guilt and shame.

THE GAP REVEALED IN OUR GOSPEL

I have found that the transformation gap is best illustrated in
the message we communicate when we share the gospel. And
even more significant is how we tell it, our tools and methods. I
believe our reduced expectations of life change comes from a
reduced gospel. This reduced gospel has impoverished and unhealthy results, both for those sharing it and those receiving it.
Several stories from ministry illustrate how the transformation
gap shows up when we try to share our faith, but that faith isn't
working for life change.

In my former church we used an evangelism program that
trained people to visit our church guests with the intent of making an evangelistic presentation. After a ten-minute "get to know
you" time, usually feeling awkward and artificially friendly, we
would get down to business and ask the unsuspecting host permission to ask a couple of questions. Never mind that these are
about the most personal questions we could ask—about a person's spirituality and relationship to God. We felt we had earned
the right to be heard through our ten-minute chitchat.

The first question, "If you died tonight, are you sure you
would go to heaven?" would be followed by a second, "What
would you say if God asked you why he should let you into his
heaven?" It didn't matter if a person was sure of getting into
heaven, if he or she didn't give the right answer to the second
question, we would proceed with our presentation, assuming
that an incorrect answer meant the person didn't know Jesus.

We could tell a person's eternal destiny by knowing them for a few minutes. That this was similar to selling soap or cosmetics door to door escaped us. So did the fact that we were reducing salvation to a kind of "deal" with God rather than a relationship with him and a community of believers.

I was getting more and more uncomfortable with it. It was "soul winning" at its best, and it led to a bragging time after we got back from our witnessing. What many saw as genuine conversions, I saw as quickly sealed deals for heaven with an assured customer as our greatest prize. What some saw as a rejection of the gospel, I came to see as a response to our offensive and intrusive behavior. Saved people were those who had right beliefs and could spit out correct theological answers.

On one of the last visits I went on before calling the program into question, the young man we were visiting answered that he was fairly sure he would go to heaven but sometimes had doubts due to his struggles with sin. He shared warmly about his love for Jesus and attempts to live for him, but he didn't correctly answer why God should allow him into heaven. His answer almost brought me to tears. When faced with what he would say to God he very seriously and yet passionately exclaimed, "Why, I would cry out, mercy!" That answer, good enough for Jesus to proclaim a tax collector justified (Lk 18:13), was not good enough for my team of soul winners.

What kind of followers of Jesus were we producing that couldn't see the life of God in someone who so obviously and humbly was giving witness to it before our eyes. He didn't have the assurance that our team was looking for. When people made a decision for Christ, we went to great pains to prove to them that because they had prayed a certain prayer and agreed with certain doctrines they were definitely going to heaven. But for much of church history, assurance has been linked to demonstrating the fruit of obedience in daily life. If there was little or no fruit, we should not be so sure of our salvation. Paul clearly expects such fruit in genuine conversion and doubts the salvation of those without it (see Acts 26:20; 2 Cor 13:5-6).

The young man's honesty was refreshing to me. His humility was more a sign of his salvation than the easy assurance our team looked for. Assurance that is based on a "deal" to take care of our sins or a decision to be "born again" is not biblical assurance. Real salvation produces evidence of constant and progressive growth in "life from above." Admittedly, we can have more assurance than the young man had. In fact, our life should evidence such progressive growth that there would be no way to mistake whether or not we are a Christian. Our life with God, even with all its struggles, should put any doubts to rest.

I went away that night convinced that our evangelism program needed to revert back to the changed lives of our people. The program for evangelism we were using was a convenient way for people to avoid change. They could witness on Thursday night and live any way they wanted the rest of the week. In fact, the leader of the evangelism program was one of those unofficial church bosses who wielded control and power over other members.

One of the evidences of our reduced gospel is the tools we use to bring people to Jesus. For many of us, evangelistic presentations such as "The Roman Road," "The Colored Book," "Four Spiritual Laws" and "Steps to Peace with God" introduced us to a version of the gospel reduced to privatized experience, just between God and me, that results in forgiveness of sins, personal peace and a wonderful plan for our life. The call to obedience or a different way of living is left to another tract or discipleship program that in effect makes obedience optional. The spiritual growth of these follow-up programs is usually defined in terms of developing habits of going to church and daily devotions, not significant character growth. Following Jesus into a radically different way of living is not part of the program. This kind of gospel doesn't reach into everyday needs, like how to love a spouse or deal with the lust, anger and contempt.

A GOSPEL WITHOUT HOPE FOR LIFE SITUATIONS

A friend mine told me about one of the many times she had been witnessed to before she came to know Jesus. The presenters had shared their tracts on forgiveness and getting to heaven, and asked her if she would like to say the sinner's prayer. She had a hard time listening to them because she and her husband had been fighting and were now talking about a possible divorce. Finally she interrupted the well-meaning presenters and told them of her marital problems, her fears for the future and her struggles to love her husband. She hoped that these people who claimed to know God would be able to help her with these problems. The presenters again offered her forgiveness of sins and assurance of heaven. This somehow would solve everything for her.

In desperation she tried to turn the conversation back to her present dilemma and in frustration exclaimed, "What will accepting Jesus as my Savior do for my marriage?" They had no answer for that question. "Just accept Jesus," they said, "and things will automatically be different." She declined their offer. It didn't seem related to her need for reconciliation with her spouse.

My friend said she has often wondered if her marriage would have been saved if someone could have shown her how God's grace applies to this life as well as to her eternal destiny. After the pain of a divorce, several further attempts at relationships, and an abortion, she was led to Jesus by a loving church community who, over a couple of years, helped her find healing. Now that she understood and was changed by the gospel, she found it odd that those who had earlier witnessed to her made no connection between God's love for her and how it could change her broken marriage.

I have been trained in premarital counseling programs that prepare couples to commit themselves "until death do us part." The training usually covers money, communication, sex and so on. However, these programs rarely teach couples how to love a spouse who has mistreated them and maybe even betrayed them sexually, but desires change.

In *Speaking of Faith*, Krista Tippet shares candidly from her own experience of divorce. She wonders if she and her former husband could have been offered more grace than they were willing to receive. She describes it as a kind of "dare from God to work things out" that she and her husband could have taken. This dare is one where we see marriage as not just a place of getting relational needs met but as a "school of love" that forms character or, if you will, a sacrament through which God's life is imparted.

What if those who claim to know God could demonstrate that kind of love to those who desperately need hope to receive love from those around them? What if we had the power to dare others to be formed in marriage rather than changing partners?

C. S. Lewis describes the challenge every marriage faces to move from a "young love" to a "great old love" in his advice to Sheldon Vanauken in *A Severe Mercy*. Every marriage starts with an immature love centered on what my partner does for me in meeting my needs. The relationship must grow or it may result in exchanging partners for another young love. The person who is transformed by the school of love will reflect God's love and be recentered on meeting the needs of his or her marriage partner. And together they will form the kind of family that will subsequently school children and others in the school of love. These kinds of families become a transformational force in society. Our life in Christ isn't just about forgiveness of sins and the afterlife, but transformed relationships, even with our spouse.

A GOSPEL WITHOUT HOPE FOR THE WORLD

Another pastor told me of his attempt to share the gospel with a neighbor in his apartment building. One day, as they were getting to know each other, his new friend asked the pastor why he described himself as "a follower of Jesus." The pastor explained that followers of Jesus admit they are sinners on the way to hell, or separation from God. We need Jesus' saving grace to get us forgiveness and get us into heaven when we die. Shortly into his presentation, the neighbor lost interest in the pastor's explanation and simply said, "Sorry, I'm not interested."

Ironically, the pastor had been reading a few books that suggested a gospel that only calls for forgiveness of sins rather than life change, and is mainly concerned with an individual's life after death and not the whole world now, is inadequate. The pastor began to expect more from his own salvation in terms of life change and a better world now. He realized that his presentation hadn't caught up with his experience with God. After a few prayerful days, he tried to talk to his neighbor again.

This time the pastor started with the fact that God designed the world to be characterized by love and goodness. The concerns that he and his friend often talked about—peace, feeding the hungry, care of the earth—could only come when a new life of love, such as modeled by Jesus, became the way of life for people on earth. His friend interrupted him and said, "Now I'm interested."

THE REDUCED GOSPEL

When we share a faith that has little to do with the needs of life here and now, we are offering a "reduced gospel." A reduced gospel does not reveal the full promise of life under God's rule and will. The root of our immaturity is found in our reduced gospels. What we believe the good news is will largely determine if we are good news ourselves. There are at least three reduced gospels at work in the church today. First, a gospel of the "right" offers forgiveness of sins and a future life in heaven with little expectation for change in the present. Second, a gospel of the "left" seeks change in societal structures but no change in individual lives. Third, a gospel of the "consumer church" offers religious goods and services in exchange for financial support and attendance, but little change is offered for life now.

I (and most pastors I know) fervently preached the gospel of the right and railed against the gospel of the left. But we fueled our ministry with the consumer church gospel. We called the gospel of the left a gospel of works, not grace. But we failed to see how our gospel of grace for forgiveness of sins didn't work for life. Our grace expected neither change in society nor change for those in the church. The best we could do was to offer religious goods and services in hopes that somehow these programs and activities were doing some good.

Looking back on those days, I realize that I had accepted a grace that left people in a mess. Our busy plans for their lives—helping us to grow our churches—didn't help that much and often added to the mess.

NOT-SO-AMAZING GRACE FOR A MESSY LIFE

Two books have helped me understand God's grace: *What's So Amazing About Grace?* by Philip Yancey and *Messy Spirituality* by Mike Yaconelli. They also illustrate our lowered expectations of life change in the present, for both publicly express their doubts that there is much more than some internal change as a result of salvation in Jesus.

God's grace, for both authors, leads to personal forgiveness and an intimate relationship with Jesus, which brings a measure of personal peace with God and relief from trying to earn God's favor. The authors call us to receive God's amazing grace and forgiveness, and they model authenticity and an end to hypocrisy. Having both worked with youth, they minister with complete honesty and transparency. These authors are very helpful, and I hesitate to be critical, but I hope that their honesty and mine will help us find what has been lost to us all.

I had first heard of Yaconelli's book when one of the pastors on my staff asked me to read it and tell him what I thought of it. With the help of a spiritual director and from reading Dallas Willard's *Divine Conspiracy,* he had begun to see progress in his life. He asked me if it was possible to stay honest with himself about his messiness and yet begin to move out of the mess into a more ordered life. Did holiness have to mean hypocrisy? Would God give us only so much grace to accept us "just as we are without one plea," or would he also make us more than we are now, more like him in wholeness or holiness? Yaconelli's idea of what is possible—honesty and intimacy, but not much real progress or growth in character—left my coworker's spiritual appetite hungry for more.

I have used Yaconelli's book as required reading in the doctor of ministry courses that I teach on spiritual formation, wanting my pastor students to be authentic in their pursuit of life change and to wrestle with whether it is possible. I require they do an exercise titled "Willard vs. Yaconelli" and reflect on the different expectations of each for the possibility of life change for Christians. Each time this is done I find they are impressed with and grateful for Yaconelli's honesty about the depth and complexity of our sin problems, his reminder of the nonlinear, zigzag trajectory of Christian growth, and the admission that his practice of spiritual disciplines is messy, a refreshing reminder of the reality of our struggle with sin.

But they are also disappointed by the book's apparent conclusion that all we can hope for in this life is to stay honest and intimate with Jesus, and that the pursuit of obedient living will result in hypocrisy and self-deception, or a form of perfectionism and works salvation. They report that God seems to "tolerate sin" in Yaconelli's messy view of growth, rather than moving toward sin's termination in this life. The discomfort these students feel neither reflects a subtle legalism, which would reduce spiritual formation to a set of rules to follow, nor a shallow moralism, which is about behavior change without a deep change of heart and character. Yaconelli's view of being at peace with a messy life does not offer a vision of a life they can give themselves to.

There is little appeal in becoming "spiritual vampires," sucking on the blood of Christ for forgiveness while being barely alive spiritually. My students recognize it often contributes to "the management of sin," an endless cycle of repetitive acts of sin and shame followed by confession and temporary relief through grace. Without an alternative way of living this sets up the sinner for needing ever more relief from sin and never finding the antidote. The students know that obedience is better than sin management. And they are hungry for learning how to put sin to death rather than becoming comfortable with it.

THE PARALYSIS OF GRACE

Lower expectations also haunt Yancey's book. Yancey asserts that God's unconditional love for us in Jesus is the key to life. And, sadly, those who claim to know this, evangelical Christians, offer little grace to each other and to those who are outside of the church. So the amazing thing about grace for Yancey is that *God treats us so incredibly different than we treat others and ourselves.* He gives examples of those who have offered this grace to others, like William Wilberforce's Clapham group, and how this affects society. Unfortunately, though, the examples are few.

Yancey continually asks why Christians don't exhibit more of what Christ came to give, life-changing grace. He never really answers the question. His book demonstrates from Paul's writings that we *should* be able to forgive and give grace, but leaves us on our own as to how to apply this information. He appears to have little vision for the process needed for a person to become graceful. Yancey seems to assume that just by passively receiving grace, we become forgiving. This helplessness is best illustrated in Yancey's struggle to help a friend who is pondering leaving his wife and kids for another woman. The friend knows this is sinful and wrong, there are no major problems in his marriage. But he feels more alive with this potential partner.

At a coffee shop, his tempted friend asks, "If I go down this road, I want to know, will God still forgive me afterward?" Yancey shares that he drank three cups of coffee while stalling for an answer. In the end he had to admit that God would forgive his friend but that it seemed an abuse of grace. He rightfully warns that his friend will be changed in this act and may not be able to repent later, but Yancey has little to offer his friend that takes him back into his marriage and the opportunity for character growth through struggle. He has no vision of C. S. Lewis's "great old love," which has learned that obedience to Christ is not only right but better and more enjoyable than sin. There is no hopeful vision of who his friend could become if he stayed in the school of love that committed marriage provides— only the prospect that his friend may not find forgiveness as easy afterward.

The book's understanding of grace is not as amazing as it could be since it offers only forgiveness and not a different way of life. Before my own confrontation with the transformation gap, I would have been just as paralyzed in responding to Yancey's friend. But now when faced with similar situations, I don't focus on the negative of sin but on the opportunity to become fully formed in Christ.

Yancey's friend was asking the wrong question. Of course God will forgive anyone of anything at any time. The question needs to be answered with another set of questions: What opportunities are there for you to be spiritually formed in your current marriage? What does your pursuit of someone more attractive and exciting to you say about your soul's dissatisfaction? Why do you think sin is better than obedience? What might your boredom tell you about your love of God and others rather than what others do for you? What about growing beyond the "young love" of your marriage into a "great old love"? What if you began to live selflessly, letting Jesus teach you and your family how to become a transformational force of love?

Certainly God can and will forgive our sin. But he will not force us to have power over sin and enjoy obedience. After his sin, Yancey's friend will need to be not only released from the *penalty* of guilt and shame, but also released from the *power* sin has over him, a power that has increased by giving it more control over his life. Worse yet, sin is diluting his belief in the power of God's grace to give him and others a new kind of life.

There is a subtle kind of paralysis that a weak and reduced grace produces in people who think they only have to worry about forgiveness and not obedience. God's acceptance of us as we are, undeserving, is only the start for his amazing work of grace in us. Truly amazing grace is reflected John Newton's and William Wilberforce's radical change of life. More than bringing about their conversion, it fueled their work to change soci-ety's most sinful practice. Not-so-amazing grace results in messy lives that are stuck in sin.

REALLY AMAZING GRACE FOR OBEDIENCE

So, what is the really amazing thing about God's grace? Is it just forgiveness from the penalty of sin? Or is powerful enough to transform people such that they can offer it to others? To do that, they need more grace than they are experiencing, the grace to become forgiving people, not just forgiven. The fact is that not-so-amazing grace, grace for forgiveness alone, simply toler-ates sin, leaves us in our mess and in sin's power. It gives no hope for becoming amazing people, those who never even won-der about trying to sin.

The acronym I was taught for grace, God's Riches At Christ's Expense, begs the question, how rich are we if we are not able to offer it to others? This kind of grace is poverty stricken. The problem with our view of grace is that we only see it as a death benefit, not as a life benefit or gift of power over sin in our pre-sent life.

Grace is, as Frederick Buechner says, "life itself." So we need grace just to live and to be, sinners or not. Each day we enjoy and each breath we take are from God's grace. Paul's appeal to grace isn't limited to dealing with a sin problem but includes our being created and sustained by grace: "In him we live and move and have our being" (Acts 17:28). And when he does deal with sin, it not only separates us from life with God but also from each other. Grace that leaves me at peace with God but in bro-ken and dysfunctional relationships with others is less than amazing.

The reduced gospel of the right, which privatizes salvation, is becoming more irrelevant to a culture increasingly aware of problems on a global scale. If we cannot go deeper than the gospel of the left, which changes only social structures, and learn a new way to live that embraces others and cares for the poor, the church will be increasingly ineffective and reduced to a ghetto of consumer churches.

THE TRANSFORMATION GAP EXPORTED

The transformation gap experience in the United States has been exported overseas. This was revealed to me on two significant overseas ministry experiences. One was in the East Asia and the other in Eastern Europe.

My first trip was to teach at a seminary in Seoul, South Korea, that subsidizes the cost of the education for international students who want to minister in the 10/40 window, an area extending from 10 to 40 degrees north of the equator and from Africa to China. I taught students from Nepal, Bhutan, Myanmar, Vietnam, Japan and China as well as a few from Indonesia, North and South America, Africa and South Korea. Unfortunately, these students had been thoroughly schooled in a reduced gospel. The idea of significant life change before death was intriguing to them.

Although many of these students had faced persecution, imprisonment and possible death for their faith, their reduced gospel was evident. When I shared how the gospel of the kingdom helps us to love our enemy, several students shared that their discipleship didn't equip them for this.

One of my students, Amos Gurang, a refugee pastor from Nepal, had his family home burned down by Hindu villagers. This tested his reduced gospel. He had accepted Jesus for forgiveness of sins and eternal life, but didn't know how to love his enemies. He shared with me how he was growing bitter and disillusioned with his faith. If God loved him while he was

God's enemy, perhaps God could teach him to love his own enemies. He and the others, many who expected to face similar testing, were hungry for a gospel that would enable them to love and forgive those who sought to take their lives.

My second trip was to the newly democratized country of Slovakia to teach Czech and Slovak retreatants about spiritual formation in the context of democracy and free markets, particularly whether we can be rich and still be a Christian. Two of the pastors shared how they almost gave up their faith during the tumultuous change from communism to democracy. Their faith no longer worked in facing the new conditions of freedom. But like Amos from Nepal, God had begun to show them that there was more to being a Christian than the forgiveness of sins and waiting for heaven.

They too had received a reduced gospel that left them practicing the disciplines legalistically and experiencing little life change. Now that they were facing prosperity and freedom, they needed help. I taught that we need to deepen our character to handle more power in life, specifically financial and political power.

HOPE FOR CLOSING THE GAP

To kindle the kind of character that God wants his servants to have, I assign the meditative exercise of reading one chapter of *The Imitation of Christ* each day. This has been my own practice over the years.

After reading and trying to practice the *Imitation* for some time, we may grow discouraged. But then we come across some marvelous words from Jesus (via Thomas à Kempis). They have encouraged me when I despair of my progress and can't see what God sees. He promises to complete his work in me and to use me for revival in his church and the world.

Fight like a soldier and if you sometimes collapse because of some frailty on your part, get right up again and with greater courage look forward to My additional grace!

Do not let your heart be troubled and do not be afraid. Believe in me and trust in my mercy. When you think you are the farthest from Me, it is then that I am nearest to you. When you think all is lost, it is then that your victory is close at hand!

2

The Double Life

How could I have become so inattentive to my wife and family in my real life while believing I was paying attention to God in my "spiritual life"—regular devotions and service to God's kingdom? And what on earth did going to heaven have to do with my present life? How did I reconcile these two lives, which seemed to make up a kind of "double life" I was living?

A few years into my discovery of the transformation gap and my journey to a new life, I experienced one of those divine coincidences in life that make me wonder if God likes to play pranks on his children, not to tease them but to surprise and encourage them with his mysterious ways and workings. He seems sometimes to be an author of a novel that twists and turns and snaps back around just in time to take your breath away. I don't think that God is playing us like marionettes, but there have been too many of these surprises in my life to think they are coincidental—or that my life isn't a coedited work by God and me!

I received a phone call from a stranger telling me he thought he might have a Bible of mine! He said he was about to throw out some books he had kept for years and found my name in an old King James Bible. I had lived in two different states for many years since growing up in Minnesota. And now as an adult I had returned to the area where I grew up, yet I didn't remember losing a Bible. He brought it to me, saying, "I couldn't throw out a book like the Bible, and something told me that I should look up the name inside the cover."

Seeing it for the first time was surreal, like a trip back in time. It was my confirmation Bible! I couldn't believe it. It had my name and the date 1968 on the title page. It even had my scribbles on the pages where I had drawn during church services.

I was given this Bible when I was being taught the reduced gospel, which produced the transformation gap in my life. As we all do, I read Scripture through a pair of glasses that filtered what I read through teachings and sermons that spiritualized calls to obedience that didn't make sense in the reduced gospel. About that time I had made several recommitments of my life to Jesus my Savior, with no idea of how to serve him as Lord. Looking at that Bible brought to mind my lifelong struggle to make sense of the passages that my theology didn't have room for.

I had to use hermeneutical gymnastics to work around the fact that God really expected us to live out the truths of these passages. Examples are Jesus' admonition not to worry in the Sermon on the Mount, and Paul's command in Philippians 4:6 to worry about nothing. That was perfectionism to me. And the goal of that idealistic passage (I had been told) was to drive us back to the cross for grace and forgiveness, not to actually attempt a life like that. Later, I would find that God didn't expect us to be perfect in this life, but there was much more of his life that I could enjoy than I had been led to believe.

For most of my life the Bible had been kind of halfway relevant to me. The first half of each of Paul's Epistles were for us, they explained grace for forgiveness, but the last half, with all the attitudinal and behavioral stuff, was not relevant. All the admonitions to pursue a different kind of life were not to be taken literally or seriously, except as ways to remind us that heaven was not in our reach.

Now, I was getting the Bible back from being a bunch of impossible platitudes. It became a metaphor for the new life God had given me.

GETTING MY BIBLE BACK

The Scriptures were suddenly coming alive in me. What had been mixed messages about some life beyond our reach, with Jesus and Paul contradicting each other—one seeming to teach a mountain of unattainable ideals and the other warning that trying to live those ideals would result in works righteousness and a denial of God's good news—became one piece. And my head knowledge was now becoming heart and life knowledge, no longer split off from each other. And this gave me the occasion to see the need to put together what had been a "spiritual life" and an unchanged "real life."

I had largely placed transformation in my "spiritual life" with my real life unaffected. Thus I lived a kind of double life. I had my devotions and considered myself to have a good spiritual life. I knew and studied the Scriptures as well as any pastor. I even memorized verses. I was very busy with Christian service and rather proud of how much I was doing for God and my church. I didn't understand why my professional and devotional life didn't have much to do with how I treated my wife and son.

But as I continued on my new journey, I became aware that I was living a double life, and I had been promoting this same life in my preaching without being aware of it. I had been asking people to attend to their spiritual lives, which meant having devotions, attending preaching and worship services, and participating in programs and serving the church. Were their real lives as untouched as mine? Did they notice that too? I noticed that when someone asks, "How is your spiritual life?" they're wondering if I have been practicing spiritual disciplines or how involved I have been with church. They're not asking about the spirit or quality of my relationships or character.

I began to see that all of life is spiritual. Splitting off religious activities as my "spiritual life" betrayed the fact that the rest of my life was not considered grounds for transformation. A person's whole life in all its dimensions needs to be transformed. We need more than church activities or some disciplines laid on top of or alongside the unchanged reality of our life. This includes our mind (thoughts and feelings), body, spirit/heart/will, and social relationships. In *Renovation of the Heart* Dallas Willard explains, "When successful, spiritual formation (or really, *re*-formation) unites the divided heart and life of the individual, that person can then bring remarkable harmony into the groups where he or she participates."

Experiencing transformation in my real life not only brought harmony into my life, but it renewed my marriage, family and church, and even affected those in my everyday world! As I began to deal with the split-off quality of my own life, I began to see the places of disharmony in other areas.

This dissonance was evident at church. While my family went to church, we didn't often have church with each other. And the church talked a lot about ministry to the world, but it was not in the world in any meaningful real-life way, in natural everyday relationships, just in spiritual activities like outreach programs. I realized that I didn't have one non-Christian friend, let alone any close Christian friends at church.

Something was wrong with me and my church. I had to start with me first. My anger, control, rage, lust, people-pleasing behavior, worry and fear, and my drivenness were split off from God's touch, contributing to my lack of harmony with others.

At best, I would confess these sins only to fall into the same behaviors over and over. I practiced this kind of "sin management," but never thought repentance and real change or mortification of these sins was possible.

Mine was the typical evangelical testimony. My conversion involved a real encounter with Jesus, some real repentance, his forgiveness and a new birth. But since I was not taught how to make repentance a life habit, thus experiencing a qualitatively different kind of life, I settled into the pattern of trying to recapitulate my first experience, often referred to in evangelical circles as "restoring your first love." Through one rededication or recommitment after another I attempted to jump-start my spiritual life all over again.

The despair and shame compounded after many such recommitments builds a sense that we are hopelessly out of the reach of God's power and love. This becomes a vicious and powerful tool for the enemy to turn us back to relieve this stress by repeating the same old sins. When we do, they become more deeply ingrained.

POPULAR VERSIONS OF THE DOUBLE LIFE

Much advice on spiritual growth and Christian living in evangelical circles unintentionally teaches a form of the double life. Why do we believe that one or two hours on a Sunday morning will bring significant change to our lives? Most remedies for sin boil down to more church attendance and a greater devotional life. We believe that church programming, small groups and Bible studies, mission trips and service at church are the ways to bring change to our real lives, but they remain untouched.

Many of the best-selling books by Christian authors on the Christian life reflect well-intentioned attempts at filling the transformation gap, but they may at times actually contribute to a fragmented or double life by giving more head knowledge and busyness or formulas that don't bring life change. They have been used to bring many individuals to Christ and to develop devotional practices, but they often fall short of a vision and means for deep character and kingdom life.

One popular series recommends being more purposeful about incorporating spiritual practices or church activities into our life. Yet these practices, even when purposely added to life, don't necessarily instruct us on how to change habits of anger, rage, lust, contempt and control. In fact, the prescription of being more purpose driven may create more driven or busy people who are not much different than before. Without a vision of a new kind of life and character, and the means to appropriate that life, our best intentions will produce more of what we already have. We develop a church-and-devotional life that merely sits alongside our real life, which remains basically unchanged.

Others have tried to fill the transformation gap with versions of the health-and-wealth gospel that concentrate on the promise of faith for kingdom success, which looks suspiciously like the American Dream, not the dream of the kingdom of God. Evangelicals, who typically don't hold these views, are unaware as to how similar to the gospel of health and wealth the immensely popular "prayer of Jabez" sounds, which asks for increased blessings of life and the avoidance of any suffering. These prayers are so unlike Paul's, who said we should be content with food and clothing, and expect to suffer loss for Christ. Suffering is the program God has ordained for our growth in character and the way to real life.

One of the most copied methods of how to do church has been the seeker movement of Willow Creek Community Church. Willow recently did a self-study, called Reveal, which analyzed their church and six others to determine whether their programs were actually producing life change. Their conclusion is that participation in church programming does not effect significant life change beyond conversion. Even teaching on the practice of the disciplines alone is not enough. The study concluded that Christians need to be involved in deep community in which those more experienced in the Christian life coach and mentor others in how the disciplines result in life change.

In the foreword to the Reveal study, Willow's pastor Bill Hybels tells of his pain in hearing from his top leaders that Willow had not done as well as they had thought in making fully devoted followers of Jesus. Bill shares that "when I heard these results, the pain of knowing was almost unbearable. Upon reflection, I realized that the pain of not knowing could be catastrophic." This kind of courageous evaluation and honesty is needed across the board in evangelical ministry if we are to reconcile our "spiritual" and everyday lives. The Willow study reveals that programs which concentrate on helping people believe the right things and offer how-to lessons on right behaviors do not produce transformed people.

The seeker movement was a well-intentioned attempt to bring church more in line with the needs of the culture, to make the gospel relevant to those outside the church. And it did just that for many churches, moving the church out of its own ingrown, religious outlook. The problem is the seeker approach is similar to a bait-and-switch tactic (ironically, a sales tactic that trades volume of sales for good customer relationships). This makes Christianity more accessible by delaying the challenging and countercultural aspects and emphasizing culturally relevant, attractive and easier life applications. Thus, seekers are set up to seek no more than a superficial version of the Christian life.

Better business principles state that customers' initial experiences condition their expectations later on. When we start with

an easier and more culturally friendly call to Christ and then try
to raise the bar later, people will resist. Encouraging people to
accept Jesus first as Savior and then trying to make him Lord
later on is a tough sell. I will never forget my first Urbana Student Missions Convention in 1973 and John Stott's declaration
that "Jesus is Lord of all or he is not Lord at all." The truth of
this statement as shown in the Reveal study is: "If Jesus is not
presented as Lord at the beginning, he will probably never become Lord."

Paul's admonition in 1 Timothy 4:7-8, "Train yourself to be
godly, . . . holding promise for both the present life and the life to
come," paints a different picture of what a transformed life looks
like both on earth and in the hereafter. His assumption is that our
life on earth should look like our life in heaven. Attempts to fill
the transformation gap with church or the American Dream reveal our impoverished view of heaven. Most view heaven as either
one long worship service with harps and clouds or as a place
where we get the life of pleasure we longed for on earth. We project our church life or the American Dream onto heaven.

THE SOCIAL COST OF THE DOUBLE LIFE

I noticed that I was split off from parts of my self that were unformed and from my family members. I also saw the fractured
and fragmented corporate life of my church. We gave lip service
to love of others, but saw little of it being demonstrated in our
congregation. But the greatest place where things were dissoci-
ated from reality was our church's relationship to the world. We
all lived in the everyday world of work, play and neighborhood,
but our church life engaged these places hardly at all. We had a
"social concerns" committee, which was preoccupied with
abortion. But working with single moms or with abortion recovery was not on our radar. And we weren't concerned with the

poor. That was a political issue. We took comfort in Jesus' misunderstood words, "You will always have the poor among you" (Jn 12:8).

Just over a century ago Walter Rauschenbusch, a Baptist minister with a heart for God and a love for Jesus, tried to meet the needs of poor immigrants in New York City. His experience led him to write *Christianity and the Social Crisis,* a classic of spiritual formation relating to the church's call to social responsibility.

Rauschenbusch called the church to become more than just the purveyor of personal morality and spirituality. He challenged the church to deal with social ills such as racism and poverty, war and robber baron capitalism. Using the Hebrew prophets' calls for justice, Jesus' Sermon on the Mount, the early church's experience, and reason, Rauschenbusch argued that human flourishing was intensely spiritual and Christian. *Christianity and the Social Crisis* still rings true today. Sadly, we have failed to realize his kingdom dream of a church that would make a difference in the world.

Rauschenbusch observes:

> One of the most persistent mistakes of Christian men has been to postpone social regeneration to a future era to be inaugurated by the return of Christ. . . . It is true that any regeneration of society can come only through the act of God and the presence of Christ; *but God is now acting, and Christ is now here.* To assert that means not less faith, but more. It is true that any regeneration of society is dogged by perpetual relapses and doomed forever to fall short of its aim. But the same is true of our personal efforts to live a Christ-like life; it is true, also of every local church, and of the history of the Church at large. Whatever argument

would demand the postponement of social regeneration to a future era *will equally demand the postponement of personal holiness to a future life.* (emphasis added)

The last sentence of this paragraph is amazing in that it reflects a presumption of change in individual Christians that we no longer expect today. It appears that when the church quit trying to transform society, it also lost hope for its own transformation and for that of its members. Sadly, the conservative church marginalized Rauschenbusch as the so-called founder of the detested Social Gospel. But he really was calling people out of a fragmented, other-worldly, privatized faith and gospel. The church's lack of social impact led him to predict the transformation gap. Today we live a double life: the spiritual world of the church ghetto is out of touch with the everyday world and all of its problems.

In 1892 Rauschenbusch and a few friends formed the "Brotherhood of the Kingdom" with the intent to reintroduce the church to God's kingdom, which embraces the whole world. They desired to see the church once again embody the message of God's kingdom and become an agent of social transformation. Rauschenbusch's work eventually influenced Martin Luther King Jr. and Bishop Desmond Tutu, and through them North America, South Africa and the world. Today there is a new stirring from pastors and authors like N. T. Wright and Dallas Willard for a new generation of brothers and sisters of the kingdom, followers of Jesus who once again demonstrate and proclaim God's rule to the church and the world. Evangelicalism needs to heed this call to wake up from our isolation from and disassociation with the world.

In the mid-twentieth century, Carl Henry, John Stott and others admitted that a soured fundamentalism had an "uneasy

conscience" when it came to social issues and the social impli-
cations of the gospel. And recently, in the hundredth-year-
anniversary edition of Rauschenbusch's book, Tony Campolo
writes, "It is hard for most current Evangelicals to understand
how our predecessors could have missed the more than two
thousand biblical admonitions to seek justice and well being for
those whom Jesus called 'the least of these.'" Instead of settling
for the religious right's angry red or the secular left's cold blue,
today's new "purple" followers of Jesus are concerned with a
fuller platform of issues.

Regardless of our politics, we need the holistic vision of transformation of society that Rauschenbusch called for. If even a
minority of the church would wake up and be the church Jesus
intended—salt and light—it would make noticeable a difference in our culture. Unfortunately, as we see in the media,
Christians are often part of the problem or their lives are too
saltless and without sufficient light to expose and stop the corruption. Where is the influence of the American church, the
most resourced and wealthiest church in Christian history, in
education, the arts, medicine, business and politics. The double
life is a great loss for our culture and world, not just the church.
And this is almost unfathomable when you consider how much
time evangelical Christians spend reading books, hearing sermons and singing songs about the Bible, the most revolutionary
social text ever written.

How do we miss two-thousand-plus verses that address social justice?

KNOWING RIGHT DOCTRINE, GETTING LIFE WRONG

Evangelicals have prided themselves on being biblical. We know
what we believe and why we believe it. And this is a good thing.
Beliefs are important. But when our beliefs remain facts, proposi-

tions and information that do not translate into life, they are not enough. In fact, we can be dead wrong in life while being right about the Bible. Most of our church programming involves teaching of right beliefs. Even our application of doctrine more often boils down to more information about what to do and rarely offers an actual plan on how to live or embody the truth presented.

Once on a trip to Jamaica I met a heavily dreadlocked Rastafarian who was peddling reggae CDs of Bob Marley. After sharing our favorite Marley tunes and looking at his merchandise, I took a chance on trying to learn more about the religious culture of Rastafarians and what they believed. I asked, "Can you tell me what Rastas believe, their doctrines?" He closed his eyes and shook his beaded dreads to the rhythm of a lyric praising "Yah," and while wagging his finger at me he sang, "Look mon, Rasta is no belief; it is a life, mon. We live the Rasta way, Yah's way." His answer woke me up to my evangelical bias toward head knowledge or doctrine rather than living of a kind of life, *a way of life.*

It is ironic that the first name of those who believed in Jesus, recorded in Acts 9, is not "Christians." Saul, soon to be the apostle Paul, was pursuing those who "belonged to the Way." Like the Rasta I encountered, Saul was seeking a group of people who were not just giving mental assent to some beliefs but were living a powerful kind of life. In fact, they were willing to lose their lives to keep it, and Saul was so threatened by them that he felt the need to wipe them out. Later these followers of Jesus would be called "Christians" (literally "little Christs") as a term of derision for their commitment to live the same kind of life as their Messiah.

There have been other occasions that have jolted me out of my controlling paradigm. One that I didn't expect happened at a conference on business practices for megachurches.

TELL THEM HOW TO LIVE WELL

I had taken my staff to a special conference for large churches that concentrated on learning best business practices. One of the speakers, via satellite feed, was Peter Senge, author of the business book *The Fifth Discipline* and a guru in developing the "learning organization," and we were eager to apply his insights on developing a culture of learning to our church. Once on the big screen he suddenly changed his topic and apologized for the switch:

> I know you want to hear about the learning organization, and hope to help you with what I have but want to share something other than the material of my book. I am a Buddhist, as some of you may know, and my tradition emphasizes how to live well. I don't presume to be an expert on your tradition, but I am concerned for Christians today that they have concentrated on right doctrinal beliefs and not on what it means to live a good life.

From his study of our Christian tradition he had concluded that we could give people help in living: "Go back and study your traditions and you will find teaching on how to live well. This is what people are most interested in. The best-selling books are mainly about two topics, money management and physical health, showing that people aren't concerned with what to believe but how to live." He spoke like a prophet, and I wondered if the crowd of conferees heard the powerful message he was bringing. Right belief in terms of doctrinal correctness was still high on my list, but I was challenged with Senge's call to help people live well and to find the lost parts of my tradition that taught it.

It rang true to what I had been reading in the Scriptures. We were trying to be learning organizations for the wrong reasons, to build big and well-oiled machines to assimilate people into our existing corporate cultures, and presumed that our current kind of life was okay, not seeing that our people needed a different kind of life, eternal life now. Bible instruction today is split off from and lost to teaching that actually shows how to live it. And we think that singing some songs about and taking some notes on the Bible for an hour or two each week is sufficient.

When we treat the Bible as a textbook of doctrines to know and rules to follow we misuse it and fall short of what God intended, a life-changing encounter with Jesus. Even worse, by doing so we might be making the Bible an idol, falsely thinking that in this practice we are becoming more spiritual, when we are really keeping God safely out of our way. Jesus told the Pharisees much the same thing when he admonished them in John 5:39-40, "You diligently study the Scriptures because you think that by them you possess eternal life. These are the Scriptures that testify about me, yet you refuse to come to me to have life."

BECOMING "LIVING BIBLES"

Could studying the Bible, even diligent and intensive study, be a hindrance to actually living in obedience to it? Could our ability to articulate doctrines and Bible teachings fool us into thinking we were somehow fulfilling them in our lives?

In a booklet I saw at a retreat center written by a Roman Catholic apologist explaining"evangelicals" to Roman Catholics, the author wrote on how study of the Bible can lead to "bibliolatry," or worship of the Bible. There is a cartoon illustration depicting the throne of God in heaven. On the throne is a big, black "Holy Bible" where Jesus or God should be. The point is that the study of the Bible can become an idol that replaces the actual worship of God.

Since the Second Vatican Council (1962-1965) Roman Catholics have emphasized Bible reading and study, admiring Protestants' command of Scripture. But Protestants are flocking to Roman Catholic retreat centers to learn simple ways of meditating on short passages in order to get the Scriptures from their heads into their hearts and lives.

Right doctrine and belief are only as good as they issue forth in transformed lives. In fact, to the surprise of many, the Bible will someday be unnecessary. The apostle Paul in 1 Corinthians 13:8 says that someday knowledge and prophecy will no longer be needed for we will know fully; we will have the fullness of experiencing what we know. We will become the Bibles ourselves. Our lives will be a perfect demonstration of what we could only imagine or hold conceptually, having become "living letters" as Paul says we are to be in 2 Corinthians 3. Did he have in mind Jeremiah's promise that the law would be written on our hearts and in our lives (Jer 31:33)?

There are three times that God "writes," and each time it is with his finger and not a pen. And what he writes on doesn't keep that well. Moses received the Ten Commandments on stone tablets. These tablets were destroyed by Moses when he came down from Mount Sinai and saw the people already breaking the law. God's engraving was quickly lost to us. As Jeremiah explained and the prophets bemoaned, the law was not in God's people but on tablets and eventually reduced to hollow traditions and rules by the time of Jesus. It was external to God's people.

Fast forward some six hundred years and we find God next writing with his finger on a wall at a party of Babylonian king Belshazzar. He was using Israel's temple vessels to wine and dine his subjects in a drunken celebration of his empire. The party was crashed when God's finger appeared, writing the words "Numbered! Weighed! Divided!" which basically meant the party was over for the Babylonians; the Persians would take over that very night. Again, the writing was lost when those walls were burned and destroyed (see Dan 5).

Finally, fast forward another six hundred years and we find Jesus writing with his finger in the sand while defending a woman about to be stoned for adultery. We can only guess at what he wrote because sand writing is not very permanent either.

The only time God wrote something that seems to stick is when God writes his laws on the hearts of his people by the Spirit of Jesus, as Jeremiah predicted he would (Jer 31:33). Paul said Christians are the letters from God that others can experience with their senses. And this is not just a symbol or metaphor, for we are to be the living Bible for others to read!

I remember when Ken Taylor's Living Bible edition came out in 1971. It was a great help to so many since it made the truths of Scripture so much more accessible for everyone. The same is true today of Eugene Peterson's *The Message*. But at best they are second best. The best Bible anyone can read is you, me and the church in all its diversity across time and space. We are God's new humanity and creation. We are becoming Bibles.

The prophecies of Isaiah and Paul foretelling this embodiment of truth in us (Is 30:20-21; 1 Cor 13:9-12) will be completely fulfilled and there will be no need for a teacher or the Bible. The promise that not one jot or tittle will not be lost and that the Word of God will not pass away is not about printed books or parchments; we are the embodiment of God's word. And we are being made so in the printing and reproduction in us of the life and character of God's perfect icon, his Son Jesus (2 Cor 3:18; Col 3:20). This makes us icons too. After all, we are made in God's image. And now in his Son's likeness we have the requirements of his law on our minds, hearts, lips, eyes, hands and feet!

A PRAYER FOR MORE THAN THE DOUBLE LIFE

A prayer of St. Bernard of Clairvaux both illustrates and calls out to God for the transformation of our everyday lives with what we know in our heads. While it is sweet to have thoughts of Jesus, Bernard notes that sweet thoughts are second best to actually being with Jesus in prayerful attentiveness. A life that leans on Jesus in obedience knows also the ease of God's good life.

> Jesus, the very thought of thee
> with sweetness fills my breast.
> But greater still thy face to see
> and in thy presence rest.

3

What Ministry Masks

How could I be so effective in church-growth methods and managing the church but so stunted in my own relational life? And if this was true of my family and me, what about the lives of those so busy working my ministry plan?

Part of my journey involved facing my own brokenness and rebellion in my family and in the church. At that time Cheri was working through family secrets and dysfunctions with the help of a twelve-step group. We both took a test in the first chapter of the book we were reading called *The Secrets of Dysfunctional Families*. This test listed characteristics of various dysfunctional systems and measured our experience of family dysfunction. To my surprise, my family of origin, a family of upstanding evangelical professional workers, was just as dysfunctional as Cheri's!

The book explained that dysfunction in family life was both "obvious" and "subtle." I found out that even though my family didn't have the obvious dysfunctions that typical twelve-step groups deal with, we had subtle issues of performance, pleasing people, control and ambition, which are rewarded in many church cultures. I found that there were many professional and lay ministers in the same situation. We are "performers" who please the "consumers" and miss the fact that most of the sheep

need more than our religious goods and services and the dream
of our organizational success.

FLUNKING THE DYSFUNCTIONAL FAMILY TEST

Once I had come to see that my everyday life was in need of
transformation and that my spiritual life was not the same as
my religious activities, I encountered some woundedness that
lay below the surface of my life. These below-the-surface issues
needed to be addressed if my life was to be transformed rather
than just dressed up in another form of the double life called
spiritual formation. Without addressing these wounded areas,
performers will turn an invitation to transformation into another opportunity to churn out behaviors without a change of
heart and life. It is amazing how we can resist true and deep
formation because of shame and denial for thoughts and behaviors in out-of-sight areas of our life, which we believe God and
others would never be able to forgive. This leads to self-rejection
and self-hatred. These toxins eat at our lives while we play
church and try so hard to perform away our pain.

And these issues inflict pain on those under our ministry. In
Soul Repair, Jeff VanVonderen, Dale Ryan and Juanita Ryan
identify three kinds of dysfunctional spiritualities: abusive, an-
orexic and addictive. These often go unnoticed among pastors
and church leaders because there is no physical harm in using
God to manipulate people and in misusing God's authority in
spiritual abuse. Leaders caught up in toxic spirituality often
leave a wake of destruction as they either chase away anyone in
their church who calls attention to the problem or move from
one church to another when they are exposed.

Sheep in these flocks are consumed by their leaders as described in Ezekiel 34:4-5, "You have ruled them harshly and
brutally. So they were scattered because there was no shep-

herd, and . . . they became food for wild animals." That is, these "spiritual" leaders are wolves who steal and kill the sheep (see Jn 10). Therefore the Lord says, "I will remove them from tending the flock. . . . I will rescue my flock from their mouths" (Ezek 34:10).

My own journey is one of becoming aware of my wolfish behavior and the subsequent transformation I underwent only to become devoured by the very wolves I had once led. I was unaware of the subtle dysfunctional issues and toxic spirituality affecting me, and I therefore was taking my pain out on those around me, using them in a sick attempt to meet my emotional and spiritual needs that only could be met by God and a loving community of his people.

MASKS HIDING AMBITION AND PERFORMANCE

As I began to face these issues in my life, marriage and family, as well as my family of origin, I found the same issues in my church's systems, especially in my leaders and in some of the congregation. There were those who looked good and yet had the subtle issues that I also had. Most of them were in church leadership, the church's "performers," along with me. We wore our performance as masks of a false identity, hiding from our real selves. We didn't know the kind of grace that would allow us to put these masks away and find our worth and identity in Christ rather than our success. "Successful" ministry rewards a good performer with attendance, giving and participation, which when ratcheted up to higher and higher expectations becomes a ravenous people-pleasing monster. One well-known pastor and preacher described it to me as "a roaring tiger that consumes with its hunger for your services."

Pastors who fall from this heap of success into sexual sin or affairs aren't partying like rock 'n' roll stars, they are almost always in tremendous pain, trying to get relief from their own self-imposed and congregational performance evaluations. After preaching, pastors wonder, *Was it as good as last time?* Before the next one they hear, *Will this one be better than the last?* The performance is never good enough. We are working too hard and our success is costing us more than it is giving back. "Success" isn't satisfying; God is. And sexual sin, which is used to reward ourselves, is not solved by going to a counselor to stop the behavior. It is a symptom of a deeper problem, an addiction to the cycle of performance, pleasing people, ambition and success. It maybe as bad or worse than any substance abuse. When we look further, it is a systemic sickness in many churches.

Another well-known pastor told me of his attempt to deal with pornography, which he used as a reward for his hard-won ministry success. He was tired of traveling miles from his home to dispose of his magazines and videos, and wanted out of the shame and guilt of his addiction. He went to several other pastors to ask for help, but only one told him he was doing wrong and needed help. The others told him he need not worry about it since his ministry was anointed and successful. Apparently God "uses" his servants just as any pimp does. The real problem behind this sexual behavior is not performance or ambition, but an identity fed by something other than simply being beloved in Christ. God doesn't "use" us this way. And this kind of ministry is done apart from God, doing things *for* God and not *with* him, and then doing the things of God *for self.*

Worship in the evangelical church is a good place to find performances both good and bad. Good performances illustrate the psalmist's admonition to worship the Lord with our hearts and with excellence. Many bad ones are performance based, but most are simply shallow, more about managing outcomes and not a heartfelt best effort.

A pastor friend of mine told me a story that illustrates how worship can be more of a performance for others than an offering to God. The worship team had just finished their weekday practice for Sunday morning contemporary worship when the worship pastor called out to Jenny, one of the worship team members, to give her some advice. "Jenny" he said, "when you hold the microphone in the services this weekend please do remember to evenly space your fingers when gripping the mic." Jenny was a great singer who consistently gave her best effort to God. So how concerned is God with how her fingers look on the mic? And what difference does this kind of ministry micromanagement make in the end? Isn't worship about the space we make for God in our hearts? But when the outcomes are based on our performance, mic finger-spacing becomes important. God's Spirit is obviously not in control, we are.

Performance at its worst is concerned with "what it looks like" and not what is going on in people's hearts. It attempts to shape worship or church in general to "attract" people to God and the gospel. It does just the opposite. It betrays a self-centered and ego-driven worship of ourselves. We sing that "it's all about you, Jesus," and yet it is about us, our success, being attractive. Will being ourselves, with our programmatic misfires and miscues, disgrace God and keep people from wanting him? Perhaps our obsession with slick and well-timed productions are well-intended, but it still betrays our self-aggrandizing agendas.

I began to make the connection to ungodly ambition when I noticed how pastors, me included, compare attendance figures as a measure of our ministry success. This ambition influences many church ministry plans and is fueled not by reliance on God but by making something happen through our own power. Rushing from one service to the other, timing the sermon to within thirty seconds of a production deadline and carefully crafting each word on experiencing the "peace of Jesus" is more than good preparation, it is trying too hard for God, not resting in his power. Cracked clay jars somehow enhance God's glory according to Paul (2 Cor 4:7).

Our church has had plenty of members with obvious problems like sex, alcohol or drug addictions. But they didn't seem as bad the habitual gossips, control freaks or those with nasty tempers—the subtle problems, often masked in false holiness, that keep churches in dysfunction. And workaholism didn't even count as a problem, especially if it was the pastor's problem. My ambition, which fueled so much of my frenzied activity, remained hidden to me until I began to question the direction of my life.

Kent Carlson, pastor of Oak Hills Community Church, has said that when you "combine the dry wood of the average consumer Christian with the high octane jet fuel of pastoral ambition, you get an unholy fire." Professional therapist Sandra Wilson has identified unhealthy patterns in church leaders, whom she calls "unhelped helpers."

> These pastors, counselors, and others have never faced their own childhood struggles and scars from childhood experiences in dysfunctional families. They are less than helpful helpers because of their own misbeliefs, inaccurate identities, disrespectful relating patterns, and distorted God concepts.

She says that it is

> essential for Christian helpers to be honest about their needs for wise counsel and/or professional therapy once they have recognized their own brokenness. If these broken areas of one's life are not surfaced and dealt with, they

lie just below the surface and are powerful influences in one's life but go undetected in attempts at controlling others and performing to their expectations.

TRANSFERENCE, PROJECTION AND WOUNDEDNESS

I discovered that my identity reflected a wound that was both unrecognized and unhealed. I was wrapped up in the psychological patterns of projection and transference as my unfaced hurts played out on those around me.

In projection mode I might unconsciously begin to treat someone as if he or she were a person from my past with whom I have unresolved issues. I might even say to him or her, "You are just like so and so," and transfer onto the person all the dynamics of that unresolved relationship. Or if I am out of control in some area of my life and am not aware of it or dealing with it openly, I may try to control others around me to get a sense of control for myself.

In a book titled *Sheep in Wolves' Clothing,* Valerie McIntyre explains that transference happens a lot in churches and religious organizations. Transference is the subconscious playing out of unresolved issues from other relationships with another person who has no part in the story. So, for example, someone whose father was autocratic and abusive will find a negative answer from or disagreement with an authority figure (e.g., pastor or lay leader) a crushing blow.

Transference is also a problem between leaders, not just with the people they minister to. Scott Peck has a chapter in *A World Waiting to Be Born* on how transference occurs between employees and supervisors, and between supervisors and board members. (It goes both ways, bottom to top and top to the bottom.) The way to diminish negative transference is to set up a therapeutic environment where there is a positive transference between the therapist and the client. This is why it is so important for leaders to attend to their own healing and get help.

Churches are ripe for transference and projection. These problems are heightened by the supercharged atmosphere of "doing things for God" and the spiritualization of problems. Instead we need to understand our problems as fallen human patterns in our organizations. Ambition is seldom detected in a system of professional and lay leaders who are feeding off each other and their work for God. Our identity and the need for affirmation is a powerful tool in the hands of the enemy. Without a strong sense of our being loved by Christ, ministry sets us up to feed off each others' egos in attempts to get what only God can give.

I felt this woundedness without knowing how it drove my obsession with church attendance numbers, comparing my ministry with my father's and other pastors'. Instead of ministry being based on my identity in Christ, it was tied up with what I did for God and how many attended my ministry. Although I knew something was wrong, I attempted to rid myself of my shame by performing better. But there was always someone or a church that was doing better. My identity also was tied up in my personal performance in my spiritual life. Doing my devotions and the number of hours I put in for the church were legalistic measures of how spiritual I was.

Through counseling and spiritual direction I came to see that my true identity is not found in the performance masks I put on but in Christ and his grace. Without healing these below-the-surface issues and the cultivation of safe environments of grace, the pursuit of the disciplines will be harmful and contribute to more performance-based and hypocritical communities.

FINDING GRACE IN THE TWELVE STEPS

When Cheri and I began our healing, we attended twelve-step groups to work through the steps that help people address the issues of denial and control in a safe atmosphere guided by sponsors who have gone through the steps themselves.

We often remarked that the acceptance and support we experienced in these groups should be experienced in the church community. Open Door was known to be such a place of grace and safety. Being authentic and vulnerable with one another were stated values of our community. But many churches are not safe. In fact when we began to go to these groups and started them in our church, there was great suspicion about them.

A counselor introduced my wife to the twelve-step group Adult Children of Alcoholics. The group helped her heal from the dysfunction she had grown up with. She learned about her obvious family-of-origin issues, discovered she was a codependent with a problem family member, and was now dealing with me and my workaholism.

I went to a twelve-step group for workaholism and for my favorite medication (very obvious and acceptable in the evangelical church)—overeating. I learned that my more subtle family-of-origin issues were almost harder to get a handle on than my wife's. A well-trained pharisee has a hard time seeing how dirty the cup is on the inside having given his full attention to how things looked on the outside.

At the church I served prior to Open Door, Cheri and I began to share with one of our couple friends what we were learning and the freedom and healing we had experienced in support groups and counseling. A friend of Cheri's was so interested she asked if she could come along to a meeting.

The twelve-step meeting they attended was a typical one. It took place in a church from which the group had rented a room for the meeting. As people arrived, they took their seats in a circle of thirty folding chairs. The person whose turn it was to lead introduced himself, "Hi, I'm Bob, a recovering adult child of an alcoholic," and everyone chimed in together with a loud, "Hi, Bob." They had obviously done this a few times before and were oddly enthusiastic about the ritual greeting.

Then there was the reading of one of the "Twelve Traditions" of this group, this one being the tradition of "anonymity." This explained that they were on a first name basis to maintain open sharing and keep the group a safe place to talk about secret things that had led to shame and destructive behaviors.

Next, one of the twelve steps was read aloud. This time it was the first step: "Admitting that you were powerless over your addiction and/or co-dependency and that your life had become unmanageable." A member who read this step aloud told a bit of her story in illustration of the step and about work she had done on the step in her life. Her painful reflection of past and present moments in which life had unraveled had many group members tearfully empathizing with the story.

The larger group broke into smaller groups for sharing about their progress or response to the first step. The leader of each small group reminded the group of the step and set some ground rules for sharing. Each person would be given an opportunity to share, but they didn't have to, saying "pass" when the group's attention turned to him or her. Cheri shared her experience with the step. She and others told of the signs that they had been codependent with a father, mother, husband, wife, child or friend. Cheri's guest passed on her turn to share—as did a couple of regular attenders.

After the small groups were done sharing, they reassembled as a big group. There were some announcements and then everyone joined hands in a big circle and together said the serenity prayer, "God, grant me the serenity to accept the things I cannot change, the courage to change the things I can, and the wisdom to know the difference." Immediately following this, they said in unison and with some force, "What is shared here stays here, the program works when you work it!"

As my wife and her guest left the building and got into the car, her friend was oddly silent. With plenty of resolve, and looking straight ahead and not facing Cheri, she said angrily, "Don't ever do that to me again."

Cheri was speechless. The dissonance between her friend's request to go to the group and these words jarred her. She had not been recruited to go. What had gone wrong? Her friend had been warned that painful things would be shared, and it might become uncomfortable. And yet, everyone had been so kind and warm to them both, as usual. And the sharing had been so powerful. What could have been so offensive? How did her friend's warm interest turn into cold hostility? We began to wonder if what we found so helpful was somehow a threat to others.

We now know the power of what is called "denial." Today, recovery culture is so popular, it is parodied on *Saturday Night Live,* is featured in programs like A&E's *Intervention* and is used in the church through programs like Saddleback Church's Celebrate Recovery. It is no longer "those people who rent space in a dying mainline church" but is one of the fastest growing programs in evangelical churches. But when we were first involved, we encountered resistance to talking about "below-the-surface" issues in most churches.

RECOVERY AND FORMATION

The healing I experienced through following the twelve steps caused me to wonder about the origins of the recovery movement and the twelve steps themselves. I knew many who considered it pop psychology and a fad. But I found the twelve steps, the community it fostered and the help of a sponsor to have a churchlike quality. How was it that my wife and I felt safer in our secular support groups than we did with our best friends at church? We also have found that within these groups there are many followers of Jesus; some are part of the institutional church and others are "spiritual but not religious," that is, not a member of a religious institution.

Psychiatrist Scott Peck commented in *The Road Less Traveled* that the founding of Alcoholics Anonymous in Akron, Ohio, on June 10, 1935, was "the greatest event of the twentieth century." Others would not go that far but nevertheless recognize that the twelve-step program is a powerful curriculum of spiritual disciplines, employing practices lost to the church such as corporate confession, self-examination and prayerful meditation for life change.

Episcopalian priest Samuel Shoemaker, an evangelical minister, was an early advocate and influencer of the twelve-step groups. If he had had his way, the two founders, Bill W. and Dr. Bob, would not have reduced sin to "disease" or leave God to "whatever you conceive," but lead a person to Christ. Nor would he have changed as drastically the form of the disciplines and steps from the originally more biblical and explicitly Christian language. Dr. Bill first experienced the power of the original and explicitly Christian steps at an organization called the Oxford Group.

Alcoholics Anonymous and the assorted "Anonymous" groups (Overeaters, Overspenders, Gamblers, Sex Addicts, and Adult Children of Alcoholics, etc.) were the fastest growing organizations in America in the twentieth century and are now common in evangelical churches. Many, like Cheri and I, would not have experienced healing and spiritual formation without these groups. This movement was the precursor to the spiritual formation movement, with recovery counselors and therapists easily moving from disciplines focused on addictions to the spiritual journey with God and others in the world.

Like so many movements that influence the church, recovery is not an addition to what God intended for the church, but actually a restoration to what the church was always about.

The church's saints are a great knowledge source regarding insights and wisdom of the heart. In *Lymning the Psyche,* Diogenes Allen suggests that these ancients' teachings and reflections on human behavior and attitudes should be submitted to scientific testing to see what of their soul care advice can be verified. For example, Allen believes anger can be dealt with by *lectio divina* or the practice of prayerful reading Scripture. He testifies to how *lectio divina* taught him to live with less anger in his life. There is increasing interest in how biblically informed spiritual formation, character development and psychology intersect—an intersection that must be cautiously traversed.

CAUTIONS ABOUT RECOVERY

Among the dangers of the recovery movement are certain harmful aspects of the influence of the thought and practice of Sigmund Freud and Carl Jung that have taken hold in some parts of the church. Evangelicals who are ignorant of the powerful practices of the pre-Reformation church have been sitting ducks for theses influences, which are subtly introduced alongside ancient practices. Leanne Payne warns that there is an influence in some retreat centers and therapies that undermine biblical formation with what she calls a "neo-gnosticism," including an occult and idolatrous understanding of how we are formed. When sin is redefined as a "shadow side" and explained as fallenness and resulting in weakness to be aware of and not deny, such teaching is helpful and life-giving. But when the "shadow" is used to embrace, excuse and indulge sin rather than eradicate it, it is a teaching of death, not life. These dangerous ideas came "when the church was largely separated from its own *infinitely superior psychology and formation* and so it was not recognized, discerned or counteracted."

Payne is concerned that this has the same effect as Gnosticism had on the early church, a blurring of the lines between good and evil, true and false, and beauty and the cancerous and parasitical distortion of beauty. This is primarily evidenced in the current dearth of writing or biblical teaching on homosexuality. In *The Broken Image* she shows throughout the book how healing is possible for those caught in unbridled lust and a syncretistic blend of paganism and Christian imagery and teachings.

SIN'S REMEDY FOR SIN

An evangelical friend of ours went to a treatment center to deal with his alcoholism, which was fueled in part by his fight with homosexual urges, and came back after a few weeks cured and sober but stronger than before in his homosexuality. Having found a new peace and joy in his life with God, he has stayed sober. What surprised us is that his counselor at the retreat center, a Lutheran pastor, had also changed his view on the sinfulness of same-sex relationships. Our friend had been offered relief from one of the main causes of the pain in his life, alcoholism, by embracing another sin, his homosexuality. He had found a way to tolerate his sin far short of the full relief he could have in Christ.

This same lack of biblical formation contributes to a culture of toleration. I found that leading my church on a journey toward wholeness meant recognizing that we had, in part, a recovery culture that was centered on self-improvement and emotional and relational health, tolerating sin, and negative toward progress in sanctification and the spiritual disciplines. A Hazelton meditation book (a great resource for recovery) was more trusted and more used by some church members than the Bible. Support groups took the place of God. And yet confronting behaviors unrelated to the group's agenda was off limits. Our recovery culture had given way in some places to a toleration-of-sin culture.

At the same time we were grateful for our recovery heritage. It continued to be part of our ministry and brought a baseline of authenticity to our values. We would ask a leader to take a break from leadership when we felt their addiction issues came to the foreground. We would challenge a performance-based volunteer's disordered need to serve, which was evidenced in doing too much or controlling others.

Before programs like Saddleback's Celebrate Recovery became popular, Church of the Open Door was one of the few churches where those with addictions were comfortable and yet challenged to begin healing. It is a source of qualified pride that a detractor referred to us in the Minneapolis *Star Tribune* as the "Church of the Open Sore." We also have been called the "Church Where They Fall on the Floor" in mockery of our openness to all the gifts of the Spirit, deliverance ministry and call for people to trust God for healing of both the character and the body. We were in a time of great transition out of the singular focus on recovery and into the process of becoming saints.

ADDICTS MAKE SOME OF THE BEST SAINTS
I believe that former addicts make some of the best saints. If strong attachments to drugs or other idols are redirected to Christ, they become powerful forces for transformation.

Before becoming a saint, Augustine was perhaps a "sexual addict." He describes his sexual life as "rolling around in chains on his bed." This is the same person who wrote that "our hearts are restless until they find their rest in God." He became a saint by trading his hunger for sex for a healthy obsession with God.

So many of those with addictions are beat up by their intense and lifelong fight with food, sex, alcohol, drugs or codependency. Thomas Green, in *Weeds Among the Wheat*, explains that those with addictions or psychological problems can take comfort in the fact that God does not look on our record of behaviors but on what Green calls our "life orientation." The trajectory of those with addictions and psychological issues can feel like permanently damaged goods, or like they have committed the unpardonable sin. Relapses and hard falls speak to their doomed fate of never finding health in this life.

Having my own addictions and compulsions, I have found solace in Psalm 130, which reminds me that God is with me in the deepest places of my dysfunction and sickness. I can trust in his Word and his unfailing love to forgive me, not keeping a record of wrongs. I can wait like the watchman over my soul in the ups and downs, victories and failings, being vigilant and never giving up until, as the psalm promises, God eventually delivers me from sin and its power. I take comfort in the advice of Brother Lawrence, who says that if I keep confessing and acting to mortify sin, it will not be able to stand or dwell in God's presence. I will either keep my sin and stop practicing God's presence, or sin will become uninteresting, boring and powerless over me. I know I cannot be helped by God without keeping before me a *vision* of life without the particular sins I wrestle with, an *intention* to be rid of it and applying *means* to be free from it. These efforts will eventually be rewarded by complete freedom from sin, maybe in this life but surely in the next.

Those who wrestle with addictions are not disadvantaged in regard to their pursuit of transformation; they are blessed. They can experience the blessing of Jesus' beatitude that those who hunger and thirst for God's kind of rightly ordered life (righteousness) may be more powerfully satisfied than those without addictions. But both will need to cultivate a strong hunger for God.

When I speak to addicts on these themes, I offer this prayer from St. Benedict. In the line addressed to the Dragon, "drink your own poison yourself," I interject, "Satan, you can drink it, shoot it up, pop it or smoke it yourself."

Prayer of St. Benedict's Cross
Let the light of the cross be my guide.
May the Dragon not be my leader.
Entice me not with your vain deceits.
What you have offered me is vile.
Be gone Satan!
Drink your own poison yourself.

STRUGGLING WITH THE DARKNESS

While I have learned that transformation may require therapy and recovery, unfortunately the presence of the demonic is often involved. Dysfunctional power in the church is not just a manifestation of fallen human relational structures but also supernatural forces of darkness. By learning how to pray, listening for and recognizing God's voice, I now have some discernment of inner voices and promptings, and am often able to differentiate God's voice from my own. I also have recognized the voice of the enemy. Temptation, shame, condemnation, excessive worry, anger and contempt signal the voice of the enemy and the hints of his tactics.

On occasion I will be dreaming something disturbing and frightening, and be surprised to wake up already saying the Jesus Prayer, "Lord Jesus Christ, Son of the living God, have mercy on me, a sinner." I will repeat it over and over until the sense of fear or dark influence is gone. Inevitably, those formed in Christ are attacked by the enemy. Whole-life formation must be prepared for the work of the enemy.

Christian warfare is simply turning from Satan's constant planting of seeds of self-destruction in our thoughts, described in St. Benedict's prayer as "vain deceits, vile offerings, and poisons" that try to turn us from Christ. But there are times, thankfully few and far between, when some are troubled by a more vicious kind of attack. When this happens, it can backfire on the enemy. The demonic assault on our culture has resulted in one of the most powerful forms of community, the twelve-step movement.

The prayer that is used at the end of twelve-step group meetings is called the Serenity Prayer. The prayer was developed by Reinhold Niebuhr and originally had more than the first few lines that are known today. The full prayer is for much more than recovery; it is a prayer for full individual and corporate formation and ends with a view of life in the new heavens and earth.

> God, grant me the serenity
> to accept the things I cannot change,
> the courage to change the things I can,
> and the wisdom to know the difference.
>
> Living one day at a time,
> enjoying one moment at a time;
> accepting hardship as a pathway to peace;
> taking, as Jesus did,
> this sinful world as it is;
> not as I would have it;
> trusting that You will make all things right
> if I surrender to Your will;
> so that I may be reasonably happy in this life
> and supremely happy with You forever in the next.
> Amen.

Church as Business

How did I get to the place where I was so off-task, caring more about my church's "organizational extension and survival" and measuring success in business terms—attendance, buildings and cash—rather than in becoming and making mature disciples of Jesus? How did church become more of a business organization for consumers of religious goods and services than a training ground for followers of Jesus?

At Open Door we faced some directional questions and decisions: Do we use our limited resources of time and energy to go for more people and multisites, or do we go deep for developing communities of Jesus? We could either go deeper with God and each other or go wider in numbers. We didn't think we could do both at the same time. Most of our staff and lay leaders were on the journey of formation together—realizing we had taken our people's and our own spiritual growth for granted and with lowered expectations. The programs we were successfully promoting were not only weak in transforming people but were also taking us from our own formation to service the felt needs of the large crowd.

Our church facilities had reached capacity, and we were at the point where churches usually add more services or went to multisites. We had to make a choice. Would we pursue our own individual and corporate transformation for a community of disciples or spend our lives managing and attracting bigger crowds of converts, hoping somehow they became disciples?

CORE OF DISCIPLES OR CROWD OF ATTENDERS?

I knew pastors who ran from service to service or from one site to another in the effort to accommodate bigger crowds. We wanted no part of that. We didn't want to hold as many Christmas services as we possibly could while huffing and puffing in exhaustion. The business metaphor that controlled most churches seemed to promote the organization more than the transformation of people. The thinking is that bigger is always better, and larger churches influence people more due to economies of scale and organizational power. But we began our own corporate journey to becoming a community of transformation. And we needed some new metaphors for what we were doing.

As I began to get at the issues below the surface of my life and found healing, I was able to review my ministry philosophy and the controlling metaphors behind it. In *Missional Church,* Darrell Guder has concluded that the primary metaphors of managers and program technicians rather than leaders that model and foster disciple-making communities has co-opted the mission of the church. These metaphors presume that churches act more like businesses that produce religious goods and services. He has made the observation that many well-intentioned pastors and leaders of Christian organizations influenced by modernist perspectives of the church growth movement have made "organizational extension and survival" their priority. The growth of the organization becomes the mission, rather than the spiritual growth of the people.

Regardless of a church's size these days, this business metaphor shapes congregations to prefer pastors who act more as managers and CEOs of entrepreneurial corporations rather than churches. Guder challenges us to find new metaphors for leadership and ministry if we are to enter into whole life transformation. I believe the intentions of those of us who have bought into the "bigger is better" business metaphor are well-intentioned. I was trying to do what I had been conditioned by evangelical culture to do. I now believe this is a powerful delusion we all must counter. But this will require some sober thinking about the condition of the church, taking it in some new and fresh Spirit-breathed directions. Our old organizational life must be abandoned for a new one.

PRIMARY ROLE: CEO OR PASTOR?

In a journal for church leaders, a prominent megachurch pastor was asked what he read to keep his ministry focus sharp. His answer reveals how the metaphors of formation have changed. After sharing that he was reading secular business books almost exclusively, he explained that he has traded the metaphor of the pastor as shepherd of a flock for that of the CEO of an organization. This begs the question, What is the business or chief activity and purpose of the pastor?

This ministry CEO understands *pastor* as more appropriate for smaller churches in which the minister is a counselor for people's life problems. His understanding of pastoring as being therapeutic counseling and not the formation of disciples may explain why he had abandoned it for the CEO metaphor. His nearly exclusive reliance on business books reveals the presumption that organizational improvement will fulfill the church's mission. This illustrates how far we have moved away from the biblical metaphor of pastors as those who care for the "cure" of souls and are creators of church cultures designed to "train for godliness" (1 Tim 4:7-8; Heb 5–6), growth into the character of Christ.

The church has lost the training model, which was first substituted by the clinical and pastoral counseling metaphor, and now the technical and business metaphor. Guder calls for those who will become designers of formational cultures and environments. To do this we need to ask how everything a church practices—weekend worship services, small congregational gatherings, small groups and one-on-one relationships—work toward the transformation of people. Biblical pastoring is not about therapeutic counseling or organizational success. It is cooperating with the chief Shepherd as undershepherds in the formation of apprentices of Jesus, guiding them into "paths of righteousness for his sake," not for the sake of organizational growth.

Supersizing McChurch

Conferences sponsored by large and growing churches abound. They package their programming success for other churches, presuming that they can bottle a successful technique and transfer it to other churches. At one conference I attended, some of the participants used a McDonald's model for church growth. The discussion centered on a one-size-fits-all program that puts everyone through the program quickly. Once they are "equipped," they are employed in service to the church's activities and mission of growth. When I questioned whether this would produce mature disciples and some in the group responded positively, the facilitator confidently redirected the group back to McChurch, asserting that "we can take for granted that we are making disciples, can't we?" After the session several pastors who resonated with my concern hunted me down to discuss the fact that McChurch isn't making disciples of Jesus. Increasingly, there are more leaders who are waking up to the lack of transformation in our churches and are no longer taking for granted that the "best business practices" are not getting the job done.

Seldom is a church program given more than one or two years before it is scrapped for something else, unless it brings numerical growth. Significant life change is expected by the end of the worship service or least at the end of forty days of intensive programming. Churches are grown in a marketing "minute" with advertising blitzes that hopefully break the 200, 500, 800, 1,000 and finally 3,000 attendance barriers, resulting in a very large church. Pastorates become stepping stones to larger ministries, where the pastor's gifts can "reach more people." The CEO or business model cannot become our primary metaphor for ministry. The dangers of focusing too much on this one metaphor must be addressed.

In a time when I wondered if God was calling me to another church, I was approached by the search committee of a very attractive and growing church looking to grow even larger. After the usual pleasantries of these kind of interviews and the questions from the committee on my experience and gifts, strengths and weaknesses, I was given a chance to ask them a question: what was their vision for the next run of the church's life. They had sent me all their mission statements and their organization's profile, and they referred me back to that material. I explained that I was looking for a picture of how the church would look different in the next ten to fifteen years. Their answer was telling. Nothing in their material addressed how the lives of the people would be changed. Nor was the church's impact on the community and the relational worlds of people discussed. They answered quite confidently, "We expect to triple our attendance, build a new sanctuary and education wing and start a multi-site." When I asked them what difference this would make in the lives of their people, they were dumfounded. Obviously, they took for granted that all this would create maturing disciples of Jesus.

I didn't even share what I was thinking: their plans might

just be too aggressive for any transformational space to be created for leaders who modeled life change. This kind of church growth, seeing it mainly in terms of bigger crowds, budgets and buildings, comes with a career-ladder mindset for ministry, which I had abandoned. My success was not measured by these quantitative and chiefly external numerical indicators but by the internal quality of growing a community of disciples who were becoming mature and making a measurable impact on the world as a sign of God's kingdom coming to earth. And that took longer than the average four or five years of ministry in one local church.

CAREER MOVES OR A LIFE CALLING?

Eugene Peterson tells of his decision to stay in one church no matter what size it grew to or problems it encountered. His goal was to stay in one church for the entire course of his ministry. He likens it to the vows of stability that monastics took when entering their order, staying put to be transformed by the community rather than trade up or out for various reasons.

One of the consequences of the church business model is pastoral careerism. From my experience it takes at least five years to get to know and earn the trust of a congregation. And to see significant culture change in the church, not just program change, takes at least ten years or longer. This is true of my experience at Church of the Open Door.

Developing a culture of transformation takes more than the typical five-to-eight-year run of most pastors. Peterson likens this to the immaturity that plagues those who leave one marriage after another when the present one is no longer gratifying. He explains that although moves are required for various reasons, "the norm for pastoral work is stability. Twenty-, thirty- and forty-year pastorates should be typical among us (as they once were) and not exceptional." And these stable pastorates are not just for the sake of the current members. They are essential for reaching the next generation.

Often, churches interested in spiritual formation do not implement it holistically but add it as a programming technique or "boutique" ministry elective, hoping it will affect the whole organization. Almost every time I am told that one person or ministry in a church is identified as *the* formation pastor or ministry, I find that the whole church has not made formation the center of the church. We cannot put transformation in only one part of a person's life or activities. It must be the heart and interior life force that drives everything in a person's life. This is what it means when Jesus says that we must lose our present life for a new one.

The same goes for the church. A church centered on the formation of disciples will need to lose its current corporate life for kingdom life. And it starts with those in charge, the senior pastor, the leadership teams and then those in every part of the church. But the key is that it takes hold in how our people, from adults to infants, are trained in formal and informal curricula for Christlikeness in their everyday world.

PAUL'S TRAINING METAPHORS

The Bible offers several metaphors for our consideration. Paul's athletic metaphors for the spiritual life involve intense and extensive training and competition for three sports: long distance running, wrestling and prize fighting. These all presume a different approach than the assembly line, manufacturing and consumption aspects of big business. Paul urges us to train for godliness (1 Tim 4:7-8) and calls Timothy to be an example of what a trained spiritual athlete looks like: it is more organic than organizational and presumes coaching, one-on-one rela-

tionships and intensive and individualized training in learning
life skills. What comes to mind are the great athletic programs
in which coaches teach and conduct practices to form habits.

Paul also used metaphors from agriculture, the military and
travel. Timothy is to be like a good farmer or soldier who is faithful over time. He needs to be careful that he's not shipwrecked
on the journey home. These metaphors speak of life's duration
and even pain, going through deserts and dark nights of the individual and corporate soul. They fly in the face of the quick
fixes offered in church seminars, self-help sermons and motivational worship experiences. Being more organic than organizationally based, the metaphors move us toward more relational
and adaptive kinds of order for our communities and leadership
training than the programmatic and linear business models do.

One metaphor views the pastor as a trainer in long preparation,
and in another the pastor is a farmer working through long seasons of plowing, sowing, watering and finally harvesting. Pastors
are sergeants with soldiers in battle, wounded to tend and ground
to occupy. They are captains of a ship of sojourners. Alternatively,
they are pioneer leaders with whole communities weathering
mountains, valleys and deserts on a long journey or quest.

These metaphors have been picked up and expanded on
throughout church history. In the East, John Climacus (author
of *The Ladder of Divine Ascent*, the most read book besides the
Bible in the East) wrote of climbing a ladder to see the uncreated
light of heavenly character and running a cross-country race of
the soul to maturity. In the West, John of the Cross (author of
The Ascent of Mount Carmel and *The Dark Night*) also wrote of
climbing but likened it to scaling a densely clouded mountain-
top where those at the peak can trust God only by faith, not
their senses. He pictured mature faith as confidence in God in
spite of our walking daily in the thick darkness of our mundane

circumstances (life with God often being like sitting in a pitch black room with someone who you know is there because he occasionally clears his throat).

Modeling, apprenticeship and mimicry are another set of biblical metaphors for formation. These call for developing close relationships through intensive life-on-life interaction over long periods. Paul said to Timothy, "you know all about my life, my sufferings" (2 Tim 3:10-11). Timothy had witnessed all aspects of Paul's life over long periods of time and his formation was more caught than taught.

This apprenticeship approach has powered transformation through much of church history. Today, however, terrorists know more about this kind of training for transformation than the church does. We have lost this tradition, what some call the "catching force," and the inherently stronger life it organically imparts through the Spirit.

ATHLETIC TRAINING VERSUS CHURCH TRAINING

In explaining the difference between the business model of the mass production of disciples and the organic models in Scripture, I often refer to the kind of training received while preparing for an athletic event. In his first letter to Timothy, Paul relates training for godliness to physical training of the body in this life. What kind of training do our people receive in most churches? The average Christian attends church twice a month for an hour of inspirational teaching or preaching and some singing. I wonder how athletes would do if they received a similar training regimen.

"Training" in 1 Timothy 4:7 is the Greek word from which we get *gymnasium*. My brother was a wrestler and I was a soccer player. Each night after school my brother would labor in the gym to practice wrestling moves and holds. I would run five miles a day to be ready for the soccer game. These activities were supplemented by how we ate, slept and managed our schedules and relationships. Basically, training took over our lives. And we were mentored by coaches and the better players.

How would my brother do if his training comprised listening to a great talk on why and how he should compete in wrestling and then sing a few songs about wrestling? His chances in a wrestling meet would be slim. Someone might protest that I am comparing apples and oranges, a weekend experience in worship with a sport. But the comparison is Paul's, not mine. Obviously, his idea of training is much more involved than ours. It was life on life, disciplined and rigorous.

Imagine a bunch of ducks going to the First Church of the Glories of Flying once a week. They waddle to church to hear sermons and sing songs about flying, and then waddle back home. They waddle throughout the week and return to the church for another dose of lessons on the glories of flying. But they have no intent of flying, nor are there any actual flying lessons. The ducks have attended church for so long that they are under the delusion that they know how to fly because they hear and sing about it every week.

Tragically, most Christians and their trainers think they are "flying." Something is wrong. But what? Could it be that we have reduced transformed living to listening to sermons of nearly useless information and singing nearly useless motivational choruses?

Perhaps our best defense against terrorism would be to infiltrate their ranks and teach them how we train people in the church. Surely it would render them nearly useless.

FAILING THE FRUIT-OF-THE-SPIRIT TEST
In his book *Experiencing Leadershift,* church consultant Don

Cousins, formerly of Willow Creek Community Church, writes about "the success heresy," thinking that God cares more about what we do for him than who we are becoming. During a four-month break from ministry, God spoke to him, telling him that he had spent twenty years on "doing" that had left him empty and exhausted. In an inventory of his life using as his bench-mark the nine fruits of the Spirit (Gal 5:22-23), he found that he had two out of nine, and those he had—faithfulness and self-control—had been more about his temperament and family values than God's fruit in him. God shifted his attention from doing things for God to being *with* God, more as a son enjoying being with his Father than just a servant doing things for him, a pruning that would bring more fruit.

I have taught on spiritual formation at conferences and retreats for pastors, many of them being from small to midsized congregations of five hundred or less. Many of them have been programmed for high stress by the expectations of their congregations to repeat what they see in the megachurches. This robs them of the kind of life they could have. And this is compounded by conferences that extol purpose-driven or seeker-friendly formulas for success that only leave them more driven and disillusioned than before.

Instead of learning to listen for God's call and unique work in their lives, they try to copy what God has done in successful churches. Their discouragement and lack of confidence that God could use them with what they have and who they are saddens me. It is very fulfilling to see them come alive in the Spirit when they realize that God is big enough to do what he needs when they partner with him as "the" program.

Having been the pastor at a megachurch, and having friends at many of these large churches, I know that the leaders of these churches are frustrated by those who copy their methods and programs without applying their spiritual principles. The problem is that a notebook, even one full of good principles, does not form people. The changed lives of the pastor, leaders and a few laypeople are the untold story that is forgotten or taken for granted.

NO LONGER BUYING THE CONSUMER CHURCH

While on a planning retreat with lay leaders and pastoral staff, a friend was using Lyle Schaller's book *The Very Large Church* to examine how to keep their church growing in numbers. The book's thesis is that churches often begin to decrease or plateau in attendance due to "failing to act according to their size," reverting to doing things as churches do. But the leadership had begun to measure not just quantity in attendance but also quality in changed lives, particularly their own. They had a kind of revival when they rejected the advice in the chapter titled "The Consequences of Consumerism," which said a church had to accept consumerism and base church plans accordingly. After much prayer and soul searching, they decided that if rejecting consumer Christianity meant a smaller crowd, so be it.

I attended a conference called "The Very Large Church" for churches with a weekend attendance over one thousand. But it also had special, by-invitation-only meetings for the churches with attendance over three thousand. Though it wasn't explicitly stated, the presumption was that bigger is better. This was evidenced by the fact that we were grouped according to size, church staffs with attendance of three thousand or more met together, and those with one to two thousand in attendance met separately. At one meeting, the two groups joined and the larger churches were asked to share their ideas with "smaller" churches. Obviously, size was evidence of success. The quality of discipleship was taken for granted.

As part of our attention to making disciples and not just getting a bigger crowd, I had our staff to ask themselves and their conference teams two questions: How would we know if we are making maturing disciples of Jesus? and, Are we making any real difference in the world outside of the church? To the shock of my staff, when the group took suggestions for topics to discuss and then voted on which ones to include, the others were not concerned with these two questions. They assumed that everyone was accomplishing the goals behind these questions. My staff were amazed and discouraged, but more determined than ever to keep on asking these questions of our church.

David Fitch, author of *The Great Giveaway: Reclaiming the Mission of the Church from Big Business, Parachurch Organizations, Psychotherapy, Consumer Capitalism and Other Modern Maladies,* raises the question of whether the people who start churches trade away meaningful relationships and transformative interactions for the business of servicing a larger organization. Although his bias is for small congregations, his point bears merit. The larger a church grows, the harder it is to keep true to the mission of forming disciples and a transforming community that engages the world.

Hand in hand with the business model of ministry is the growth of consumer Christianity, which flips the church's mission from forming servants for service in the kingdom of God to managing and designing programs that serve consumers of religious goods and services. From a survey of pastors, analyst George Barna says, "Few pastors indicate that success relates to the spiritual quality of the lives of congregants. More often than not, you hear about the quantity of people participating in a group or activity."

The fact is that we cannot mass-produce disciples. Disciples are created in a community of life-on-life organic relationships.

Religious goods and services aren't the only things devoured in the consumer church, people are too. Volunteers and workers become statistics and giving units managed for the organization's success. The illusion is that this all adds up to spiritual growth. This system deludes the average member into thinking they are growing, but they and their leaders grow distant from each other and their families amidst the busyness.

The attempt to mass produce disciples usually produces a programmatically driven trinity of information, technique and motivational experience. These are not bad in themselves, but head knowledge, formulas and emotional highs cannot be relied on to make disciples. They can't replace a one-on-one relationship with a person who models a dynamic life with Christ. Evangelism and discipleship are not techniques to be mastered but are best learned in communal relationships fostered in the context of everyday life. Motivational experiences are no substitute for God's Spirit among people missionally engaged with the least and the lost on a daily basis, not just on a "ministry night" at church. As long as our mission is driven by organizational extension and survival, and entrepreneurial business is our metaphor for church growth, we will not see transformed churches and communities.

I still read business books like *Built to Last* and *The Wisdom of Teams* because there is a business aspect to what I do. I find most of these authors helpful, and their best business practices are actually quite good as spiritual practices for work relationships and productivity. But ultimately they don't help with my bottom line. While churches are complex organizations, business cannot be the controlling or primary metaphor for our leadership.

The Holy Spirit is not necessary when discipleship is manufactured and commoditized. It is a sign of our brokenness and rebellion when we think that we can do so. The work of transformation cannot be co-opted as a man-made project; it reflects the personal touch of God's Spirit calling us out of resistance and self-centeredness and into the cooperative work of repentance. When the Spirit is active, programs take their place in service to God and his church rather than serving organizational success. Results are left with God as we concentrate on being faithful to becoming his disciples and measure success in terms of obedience to him.

When we enter into apprenticeship with Jesus, our ministries may not look much different for a while as we concentrate on our own lives as the "program." In many cases the church will need the same kinds of programming for kids, adults, care, outreach and so on. The difference is how and why we do it. Are we driven to build the organization in a way that depletes us and those we minister to? Or are we concerned for the formation of others, and with doing ministry in a life-giving and restful way? The proof is in the pudding.

What if our measure of success was not determined by counting attendance numbers but by the more elusive (but still quantifiable) difference it makes in members' family life, work and leisure time activities? If their lives were seen as the church's program, it would change everything in our approach. Our approach to ministry would be much more relational and our success would be measured more by the quality of their transformational interactions with the real world. Transitioning to this form of ministry takes time. Unfortunately, due to their own career goals or to the congregation's expectations of fast numerical growth, pastors rarely stay long enough to see their churches so transformed.

LOSING THE NEXT GENERATION AND THE CULTURE
Shane, a twenty-something being mentored by the senior pastor

of a large evangelical church, wondered if professional ministry was in his future. After much soul-searching he decided he was called to work for the kingdom of God, but not necessarily in a religious context. He thought about teaching at a college, helping manage his family furniture business or even becoming a fireman. He was captured by the idea that God could more powerfully influence the world for Christ through him if he was *not* in professional ministry. When he announced his decision, he was shocked by the great disappointment and even irritation of his mentor. "I thought you were going to really amount to something in ministry, to make a big impact in the kingdom of God," the pastor told Shane, hoping that Shane would wake up to his destiny in the church—the pastor's church, to be exact, which he idolatrously mistook as his little kingdom.

Shane related this story to me with more sadness than anger. It is not the first story like it I have heard. And there is a follow-up to these stories. Frustrated by pastors like Shane's and church systems and cultures that are not working, many younger pastors are prayerfully deconstructing and reimagining what it means to be church. Some of these younger leaders are part of the emerging, or emergent, church movement. They are not interested in "going to church" but want to "be the church" with other Jesus followers and God seekers. Not satisfied with being "alone together" in the highly programmatic and impersonal factories of religious goods and services, they desire doing life together.

The fact that these young leaders have had to emerge without mentoring reveals a fundamental failure of the church, a fumbling of a whole generation of young leaders. The evangelical church has reduced God's kingdom to the petty turf behind organizational and physical walls.

The business model of the American church is not good business because it has not nurtured relationships with the next generation. The institutionally and organizationally idolatrous church fails to follow in the spirit of the psalmist's desire to "declare [God's] power to the next generation" (Ps 71:18). Formational ministry stays in community with the next generation. The mentoring relationship is a two-way street in which the blessings of power and humility are joyfully shared between the generations. How can the church successfully minister across cultures when it can't even minister to its own next generation?

THE CRISIS OF THE AMERICAN CHURCH

Three recent books examine church attendance trends and confirm Willow Creek's Reveal study. The church's failure to make disciples is growing worse each year. Based on current statistics, George Barna's book *Revolution* predicts that by 2025 only 30 percent of those seeking ways to experience church will do so in what is now the traditional congregational form of church. Many of those opting out are "post-congregational," that is, while they no longer go to church, they still have church with friends and family in an intimate setting. Barna sees the rise of more family-faith or house churches and even cyber-churches.

In *Churchless Faith,* Alan Jamieson, studying the patterns of those exiting typical evangelical, Protestant and charismatic churches in Australia and New Zealand, has found that the profile of what he terms the "churchless faithful" is a surprising mix of spiritually mature and highly trained thirty-five to forty-five-year-olds, the very people churches count on for leadership. (The North American Reveal study shows the same group of mature leaders exiting.)

The last book, *The American Church in Crisis* by David Olson, is most sobering. Research on more than half of the four hundred thousand churches in the United States documents that American church attendance is in actual decline when measured against the U.S. general population. The American evangelical church, usually growing, is beginning to see the signs of its own decline. This flies in the face of high profile megachurches and their celebrity pastors, which may give us the impression the church is still growing strong.

The final nail in the coffin is the latest report from the Search Institute on the alarming rate of young people falling away from traditional churches. It is getting so bad that America is seen as a mission field by followers of Jesus from Asia, Africa and South America. Philip Jenkins makes the case that Christianity in the Global East and South is surpassing that of the North and West, including America, the United Kingdom, Australia and New Zealand.

How did we get to this place?

MOODY, REVIVALS AND THE EVANGELICAL GHETTO

Just about the time when Henry Ward Beecher (1813-1887) was peaking in popularity in the late nineteenth century and the future inner-city pastor and theologian Walter Rauschenbusch (1861-1918) was just a kid, Dwight Moody (1837-1899), a successful shoe salesman and evangelist, was becoming famous in England and would soon come home an evangelical hero. Moody had taken the sensationalism out of earlier revival methods and implemented a cool, yet folksy, business method of his own. For Moody, evangelism was about winning souls: "I look upon this world as a wrecked vessel. God has given me a lifeboat and said to me, 'Moody, save all you can.'" He would go on to make contributions in education and world missions, with the vision for "the evangelization of the world in this generation." But that evangelization, or "soul winning," evidenced a slight but fatal reduction of the gospel, one that would result in the two reduced gospels of the right and left referred to in chapter one.

Charles Reich identifies the two gospels of right and left in what he calls Consciousness I, which views relief work (e.g., giving a meal to the poor) as a way to save souls, but ignores the social and structural evils they face, and Consciousness II, which addressed the social structures but not the individual's spiritual state. These two minds, representing the conservative "personal salvation gospel" and the liberal "social gospel" continued to grow further apart until the recent postmodern, post-liberal and postevangelical engagements of today.

Thus the church of the American Dream became ghettoized and has reduced itself to a business, offering a big box of religious goods and services. Walter Rauschenbusch's warning and prophetic insight held true: when the church forgets its social obligation, it soon forgets its call to transformation, becoming a ghost ship of souls waiting to be transported to a heaven that lies somewhere out there. In the meantime, it makes occasional forays into the world to try to win more souls.

So we build big boxes to worship in once a week thinking we are being changed by taking notes on a life unwanted and untried, and maybe giving another night or so for "serving" Christ at a church job or club.

A PRAYER FOR MY CHURCH

Lord, we don't need

More weekend services or multisites with preaching and
teaching for the same old incomplete gospel and
additional head knowledge,

More weekend worship productions for disembodied
emotional responses of the lips and waving hands
masking the same mainly unchanged and
nonworshipful everyday lives,

More 24/7 programmed church activity for a double life

that doesn't transform people in their real lives for
their real worlds but actually keeps people busy,
driven, in quiet desperation for *you*.
Lord, we need *more* of your life in our real life,
    in our life together
    in our real worlds.
Lord, we need
    More who are becoming the good news, everyday
        sermons demonstrating in our lives your life and love,
    More who worship with our very bodies as living
        sacrifices, embodied proof of your kingdom on earth,
    More whose life influence on others is the "program,"
        by the catching force of a real difference seen in us
        not perfect, but being perfected and glorifying *you*.
Lord, We need *more* of your life in our real life,
    in our life together
    in our real worlds.

Interlude

Dad, How Do You Stop?

Kyle's question "Are you home yet?" had slowed me down enough to see how driven and empty my ministry and life had become. My whole life needed transformation, which would involve lessons in slowing down and stopping long enough for God to lead me into change.

Slowing down and stopping are critically important to life, and we need to learn how to do this early on. It's similar to teaching my son how to stop when riding a bike.

Kyle had mastered riding with training wheels and was eager to try two. Helping him learn to balance himself, with one of my hands on the back of the bike seat while running alongside, was all the preparation he required. That sparkling blue Schwinn bike with the chrome handle bars was not exactly a Harley, but it went fast enough for a five-year-old to be simultaneously scared to death and higher than a kite.

After some false starts and a few erratic swerves that just missed a couple of neighbor's mailboxes, he eventually got the hang of controlling the bike. He made a few more runs and was gaining speed and confidence. Soon enough the side streets of our little neighborhood were his speedway. Doing several laps and each time looking a bit more sure of himself, I began to wonder if he would ever quit and give it a rest.

Then I noticed that he was not so sure of himself. The anxious look on his face grew more serious with each lap. Something was wrong. Suddenly, he ran the bike up the curb and onto the grass in front of our house and leaped off, tumbling head over heals, while the bike careened to a halt.

I ran to him to see if he was okay, and he looked up at me and said, "Dad, how do you stop?" He had known how to use the brake when still on training wheels, but in the rush of being free of the constricting training wheels he forgot what he used to know how to do. So after another lesson on stopping and several more crash landings, he eventually remembered how to slow down and stop.

My first years in ministry looked a lot like Kyle's first bike ride. Hooked on the fast pace of ministry, I got dangerously out of control. It took a crash to help me slow down and learn to stop.

5

Formation by
Family and Friends

Ｈow would I make my way home to Kyle, my family and God? How could I stop my current pace of life and slow down to live a different one?"

As a young minister I found ministry to be an exciting ride. The pace of ministry is really fast, and before I knew it I had forgotten how to stop. (Actually, I had never learned to stop in the first place.) God used my family to get my attention. The same little boy I taught to stop a bike helped me to stop a life that was about to miss him and my loved ones. I needed to stop and be formed with help of some new friends, one a therapist and the other a spiritual director, but the most help I got was from my family, who called my attention to them and to God. Formation primarily happens in the space that exits with those closest to you.

Upon hearing my story, Susan Phillips, author of *Candlelight: The Art of Spiritual Direction,* said that we often miss the importance of ordinary relationships—such as our families and friends—in our formation. In her book she shares how all her relationships, even with those she directs, are formational in her own life. She receives as well as gives. Relationships are not one-way streets. Are we friends or strangers to those who see us most and probably know us best, our spouses, children and friends? If they are strangers to us, how can we receive the gifts God has for us in our formation?

What an irony. We have led all kinds of programs at church, even ones on formation, but we don't allow our own family members and friends to help form us. While Phillips was visiting an ancient temple site on the island of Malta, a guide pointed out a small booth in the wall at the entrance to the temple. In this booth a priestess would encourage visitors to stop and share what was troubling them before going to offer worship or service to God. Our families can serve as our "holy listeners," helping us discover what is going on in us spiritually. Kyle's question to me, "Are you home yet?" stopped me in my tracks. Like the priestess, he helped me to identify what was troubling me and stopped me from my unexamined life of service to God.

As John Henry Newman observes in his sermon "Love of Relations and Friends":

> The real love of man must depend on practice, and therefore, must begin by exercising itself on our friends around us, otherwise it will have no existence. By trying to love our relations and friends, by submitting to their wishes, though contrary to our own, by bearing with their infirmities, by overcoming their occasional waywardness by kindness, by dwelling on their excellences, and trying to copy them, thus it is that we form in our hearts that root of charity, which, though small at first, may, like the mustard seed, at last even overshadow the earth."

MINISTRY THAT KEEPS GOING AND GOING
Stopping is essential to staying healthy in ministry. Like so many who have had an initial experience of God's intimacy and

love, I headed into the "work of the Lord" thinking that I was invincible. I did not realize that working for God can become a substitute for being with him. A sure sign that our life is not being wholly formed in all aspects is the inability to stop and be with those most important to our formation. We are too busy with all kinds of things that keep us from the center of our life, where God and others are. My first stop was my son's penetrating question. He helped me to look at my life, and it wasn't pretty.

I was like the Energizer Bunny—I kept on going and going and going. The attempts I did make to stop were actually rolling stops, the kind that will get a ticket from the police. I never really stopped. I just slowed down enough to get going again. Ministry will not turn itself off. People's needs are always there and so the work of ministry is never done. Success in ministry, if that means more people at church, does not necessarily bring any more relief. The next sermon needs to be better than the last, so we worry about it more each time, starting on our day off and finishing the day before it's presented. We never seem to get off the sermonizing wheel. I know I am obsessing on my sermon when I am constantly waking up to write down a thought in the middle of the night.

Then, there is the "pastoral presence" that is essential for anything at church to work well. We hear it time and again: "This church program needs the pastor's presence and participation if it is going to be a success." Who made that rule? It took me a few years to realize that I did not need to be on every committee. In the meantime I went to many planning sessions, kickoff banquets and "show your face" appearances that I now think were unnecessary. If I was not there, however, I was worried about whether or not I was losing control or influence. The success of the church was largely on my shoulders. My performance was key to the church's success. That weight was something I loved and loathed. It fed my ego and also drained the life out of me.

I did take time off, but my days off or vacations were not restorative in the way they are now. Days off seldom were relaxing—more like catching my breath to go in for another deep dive. Mondays found my head still in the pulpit, reviewing and critiquing yesterday's message and beginning to tease out the sermon idea I had for next weekend. If it wasn't the message, I was consumed with the ever-present church contrarian or complainer who had gotten my goat. He or she became an invisible conversation partner who was more present to me than my wife and kids. Cheri got so good at discerning this that she developed a habit of calling me out, asking, "Are you still at church?" To which I would answer yes, explain what I was preoccupied with and try to focus on her and the kids. But more often than not my mind and heart would drift back to "church."

LESSON 1: PASTORS NEED THERAPY TOO!

I asked a trusted friend and therapist what he thought of me going for some counseling. I needed a counselor who didn't know me or anyone in my circle of relationships. He gave me the name of another counselor. I called a few days later, nervous and embarrassed and feeling like quite a failure to have to go to these lengths to find help. Counseling was something I prescribed for messed-up people who couldn't make their lives work. It wasn't until I needed to consider counseling that I found how proud I was and how out of touch I was with my own humanity. But this condition was not just my own creation, it was supported by those in my church. Pastors, in my circles and at that time, were not supposed to need a counselor. They should have their act together.

Part of the pain Cheri and I experienced was the rumors floating around about "our pastor and his wife's problems," and our being somehow unfit for ministry. This was generated by the fear of counseling and therapy in some evangelical circles. Many believe that people who need counseling must be unspiritual—and it is totally unacceptable for pastors. There was an incredibly high and narrow pedestal they had me on. And I was falling off it by going to counseling. It was okay for me to suggest it to others, but to need it myself was a little too human for them to handle and a sign of weakness. Their fear of my weakness was a projection of their fear of their own weaknesses.

My first visit to the counselor was one of the most frightening experiences I have had. I have a fear of heights. One time on a trip to Israel I walked on a steep path over a deep *wadi*. I found myself "hanging" over a three-hundred-foot desert valley near Jericho and experienced a terror that only was matched by my trip to the counselor, where I stared into the depths of my deep heart and its seemingly fathomless crevices.

I wanted to bolt when entering his office but was too desperate to do so. After asking me why I had come to see him, the counselor had me share my life in blocks of ten years starting with what I could remember from my childhood. I told him of growing up as a pastor's kid and my struggle to be seen as normal by friends at school. Then I proceeded through my years of college, seminary and church ministry up till Kyle's question, which occurred a few weeks earlier. The counselor didn't say a word for the whole hour. I had no trouble sharing. In fact, as I talked I became aware of feelings of anger and hurt over some painful incidents that were in my memory but not unpacked emotionally. I was surprised at how these issues were touching me so much. Gradually, during that hour, I let my guard down. My head and heart had been in a battle for control before, and during that session my heart won out. I stopped using my mind to shove down what was in my heart.

On the car ride home, a long drive because I made sure this counselor was nowhere near where I lived and worked, I began to cry. And the crying grew into a flood of tears, sobs and loud sighs lasting for the hour's ride home. When I told my wife about the session and the ride home, I realized that I had not cried like that for maybe five years or so. This release of years of pent-up emotion and pain had a cleansing effect on me. Although still anxious about being found out as a messed-up pastor, just letting out all those emotions allowed me to experience a kind of peacefulness and rest. And I began to look into my family's formation.

"The rake story" about my grandfather and father has become a symbol for me. It was fall and my dad's father was raking leaves in the backyard. So my dad went out to help him. But more than just helping him, he wanted to simply be with his dad. When asked if he could help, his dad said nothing and handed him the rake and went off to get some other project done. The moment became a defining one for my father. He never asked to do anything with his dad again. The message was clear. Work is more important than relationships. Getting things done as quickly as possible is the best use of time.

My father's story became my story. Ministry became a kind of rake for my father that removed him from his family. And I repeated this pattern in my own family.

As I learned to stop for the relationships in my life, the story of the rake has haunted me. Have I handed my family the rake and not given them me? Do I put work, even "the Lord's work," ahead of them, as confusing as that is.

During a tough time in my adult son's life, he was barely making ends meet financially. He lived across town and I was very busy with ministry, so we had a hard time connecting. He called my wife to ask for some money for new shoes. While my son waited for an answer, Cheri and I discussed what we could do for him. I said I had some extra money that I could mail to him. (I had several important appointments that week.)

And then it hit me. Here was an opportunity to be with my son. Instead of just mailing the money, I would go shopping with him for the shoes and we would go out for dinner afterward. Mailing the check was easier and cost me less, but it was the equivalent of my grandfather handing Dad the rake.

For those of us with families of origin that valued work more than relationships, ministry is a set-up not only for passing down a dysfunctional way of relating to work and family, but actually blessing it as pleasing to God.

LESSON 2: FINDING MY LIFE AS MINISTRY

Counseling led me to confront issues in my marriage that came from having an affair. Not one with a woman but with the church. In the process I also faced my need to control, people please and perform, all which proceeded from my ambition to have a large church. I changed enough that those who had joined me in this affair were not happy when I did not play my part anymore. They literally told me, "We want the old Keith back."

I didn't care about the numbers anymore, and even though the church was now growing as never before, this group of original founders were losing control and "took the church back" through a kind of ugly corporate takeover. I resigned rather than fight. I really thought ministry was over for me. My year off allowed me time to more fully discern that I had been ministering from what Judy Hougen has identified as the false selves of people-pleasing, performance and control rather than my true self, my belovedness in Christ.

In the year that I left ministry I received a birthday card from my grandmother, who was very proud that her son, my father (a very successful pastor and seminary president), and now also her two grandsons, were pastors. She meant well. Her card, written by her own hand, contained an outline of most of the book of Jeremiah, recounting his attempt to run from God's call and applying it to me. What she said made it almost impossible to find where she had written "Happy Birthday." The card was a symbol of how my identity had become too enmeshed with what I did in professional ministry. The year off was a hard one of settling my identity in Christ alone and not my history as a pastor's kid or as a successful pastor.

I knew I had done some good work when I realized one day that I still had a ministry—my life, not my job, gifts, career or being in the "ministry." I now teach pastors that formation is essential because our life is our ministry and our ministry is our life. Although gifts, office and call are important, they are not as important as the authority of our life and its transformational power. In my ministry to pastors and leaders at our church, this is a great leveler between clergy and laity.

Since this lesson, I have been on guard against seeing ministry as a source of my identity or of those in ministry around me. Success in numbers, acclaim or popularity cannot define us. I have a post-class project in one of my courses that has students examine their current rule of life—what they currently have as practices, relationships and responses to life experiences. Then they examine how this reflects their vision for the kind of life they want to lead. This is not limited to traditional spiritual disciplines. I want them to intentionally look at what is currently forming them for good or bad (e.g., their use of the Internet) and then change their rule for a new kind of life and ministry.

LESSON 3: NEW LIFE DIRECTION FROM SPIRITUAL DIRECTION

In a doctor of ministry program during the summer of 1995 at my seminary, and in one of the few courses offered in spiritual formation, I was encouraged by the instructor, Dallas Willard, to prayerfully inquire if spiritual direction was right for me, and if so to seek out a spiritual director. I knew of no evangelical spiritual directors at that time, nor were there evangelical retreat centers near me. So I found one, or rather, stumbled onto one, at a nearby Roman Catholic retreat center and began a program of informal spiritual formation with Father Jim Deegan, a Jesuit-trained priest. I am forever in this wonderful man's debt for guiding me into a life that Dallas Willard helped me get a whiff of.

Father Jim said that the only requirements were that I really wanted to know how to pray (but it was okay if prayer was a struggle) and that Christ and the Scriptures would be our focus. When I asked about his views of God's grace and Christ's work on the cross, he said that this whole process was totally dependent on Christ's mercy and grace—it was not our work—but does involve our cooperation with God's grace for progress in holiness. I went on to receive direction from Father Jim for nine years, and although I have moved on to other directors, we remain in contact and he occasionally meets with me. He became a true spiritual friend, not just a professional director, one who has grown to know me and can read my soul. I find that this kind of soul care through a soul friend is essential to being healthy in ministry and open to God. I cannot do this on my own. And I need someone outside of my faith community to help me discern God's voice.

This is what spiritual direction is all about—finding someone who will come alongside to help us hear God and notice God's promptings as we journey through life. A spiritual director must be someone we trust enough to be in the same room with us when we open up our heart to the heart of God. Someone who we know will gracefully tell us the truth in love, the truth of what they see in our life, who can do so because they too have an openhearted and openhanded life with God.

Spiritual direction is variously defined as "the gift to be sensitive, present and supportive to the spiritual journey of another" or "holy listening." Eugene Peterson explains that

> the problem with the term spiritual direction . . . is that the words themselves are misleading. *It sounds like you're giving direction to somebody and you're not. And it sounds like it's very spiritual, and it isn't. It's very ordinary and it's more like a mutual quest. You agree that certain things are important.* When I go to my spiritual director, the one thing that's most significant is that I know that she believes that God is the most important part of my life and that prayer is the center of what we're doing—and that's all. It's a re-centering on primary concerns.

Spiritual direction is a key to my becoming a disciple of Jesus. My former discipleship experience came from programs like the Navigators 2:7 Series and the "Timothy" program of the Christian Business Men's Committee, both of which tend to be about learning doctrine, Scripture memory, witnessing and stewardship. We did Bible studies on and memorized verses about prayer, but did very little of it. For all the meetings and study, the discipling relationship and our lives were not bathed in an atmosphere of prayerfulness. We weren't very open with each other either. Our relationships were built around accountability for completing lessons, memorizing Scripture and praying about superficial things.

Even though this now appears inadequate when compared to

the discipleship of spiritual direction, I highly value what I received through these programs and was able to pass on to others. But I also think we can offer new believers and disciples a much richer experience.

When I first read what Peterson said about spiritual direction it sparked interest, but I didn't follow it up with further study or interest. At that stage in my life it seemed strange and too serious to me. It also was too honest for my spirituality at that time; that stuff was between me and God. And if I needed to, I could always see a counselor. That was during a winter of my soul. My spirituality was a mixture of twelve-step practices, journaling and prayer based on old and worn methods from my Navigators and Campus Crusade for Christ days. I used the Scriptures like I used the twelve steps, more an introspective search for well-being and help for my personal problems than for meditative reading and listening prayer.

Looking back, I needed the depth of recovery's *heart* emphasis but without the therapeutic focus on me and my problems. I needed to focus more on God and my walk with him. I was talking at God, using wooden praises and lists of confessions and petitions, not conversing with him. I was telling God things but not living a life of prayerful listening—I needed less praying with my head and more with my heart. At the time, I didn't know what I needed; I just knew I had no real and substantial way to go to God. There *were* wonderful times of connecting with God, but they were few and far between. In between were long stretches of prayer that amounted to introspective talking to myself. I felt confused about this and found it more and more difficult to pray.

Prayer was rarely eagerly anticipated. As soon as I tried, I was barraged with scattered thoughts and found it hard to not get going with the business of the day. When I did press on in prayer, I was at times richly blessed. But this was difficult and hard to duplicate. Looking back now I see that I didn't know how to still and quiet my heart (se Ps 131). I didn't know how to practice solitude.

When I first heard of spiritual direction, it seemed exotic, strangely mystical—something practiced in monasteries. But it's not. Anything truly spiritual has a mystical quality, but we don't need to be a mystic to be in spiritual direction. Spiritual direction examines the events and relationship of our ordinary life and helps us develop habits that make ordinary life spiritual. Here is where I have been taught the disciplines of solitude, listening prayer, meditation and fasting. From the baseline of these habits has come a peace and consciousness of God in life that I never knew before.

Under the guidance of my spiritual director, I feel free to bring up my deepest moral and spiritual questions and struggles—about relationships, money, time, decisions, gifts, career and calling, and passions. Typically, I look deeply at these only in times of crisis. Yet they are the most important things in my life and require my attention. Now they are at the forefront instead of being forgotten in the daily grind. And when I feel this sense of spiritual living slipping away, I have a place to go to recover it.

I believe we need to do as Eugene Peterson suggests:

> In the best of all possible worlds, no pastor would "get" a spiritual director. We would already have one—not by choice or inclination, but by assignment. For the very act of choosing a spiritual director for ourselves can defeat the very thing we are after. If we avoid anyone who we sense will not be tenderly sympathetic to the dearest idols we have known and opt for conversational coziness, we have only doubled our jeopardy. But we don't live in the best of

all possible worlds, in which someone looks after us in these matters, and the vocational/spiritual peril in which the pastor lives is so acute that, dangerous or not (but very mindful of the danger), pastors must get spiritual directors. Our sanity requires it.

LESSON 4: FORMATION BEGINS AND ENDS AT HOME

Once Cheri and I began to live in different patterns, she began to face significant areas of her life where she needed healing and growth. Her family stuff had caused her to be very cautious about opening herself up to trust in others. And she had thought that being a pastor would make me a better husband, but her hope turned to despair when I proved to be worse than her friend's husbands. So I resolved to woo her again.

The hurt of our marriage's early years was now gone. We were closer than ever, but now it was her turn to do some soul work. She could easily pour herself into her friends and work, which she had done before we started to work on our marriage. In *The Meaning of Persons,* Christian psychiatrist Paul Tournier says that the freest person is one who has told his or her life story to another.

> The man who keeps secret his most painful memories, his bitterest remorse . . . must needs show also, in his whole demeanor and in all his relationships with other people, a certain reserve which they all intuitively feel. This reserve is contagious and sets up an obstacle to the development of personal relationships. On the other hand, the liberation experienced by the man who has confessed his sins is also contagious, even if he says nothing about the burden that has been lifted from his shoulders. All who come into contact with him find themselves becoming more personal.

The healing I experienced created a new atmosphere for both of us to explore. But it took some very intentional effort on my part to do so without reverting to the old control and manipulation mechanisms I had learned. I began to send Cheri cards, romantic cards that conveyed my desire for her and the deepening of our relationship. I wanted to put Cheri first and to work at creating a relationship that reflected Christ's love for the church.

In the corner of the envelope where the return address goes, I would put the obscure "A Great Old Lover," reflecting our mutual desire to have the kind of mature love described by C. S. Lewis. These cards came to become a favorite of Cheri's, and I still send them at times to refresh our relationship.

One day Cheri, a teacher, reported that the office talk at the school was that she was having an affair. Apparently the office mail is not too private, and someone had seen one of the "Great Old Lover" envelopes. How ironic! I went from having an affair with my church to my wife's coworkers' thinking she was having an affair. This time, though, it was a good one.

Our marriage grew as I became less consumed with success at church and more available and present to my wife and family. We didn't just pass by each other, living on the surface of life, but developed habits of being together at the core of our being.

As I became available to my family, I noticed their needs. For example, my daughter, Cara, had begun to exhibit some speech anxiety. As a middle-school student she was starting to make oral presentations in class, which she found very difficult. Cara was confused why God didn't answer her prayers and just take away the sweaty palms and the red face, the panicked feeling that shut her down.

I asked Cara to consider that God might actually take her through this rather than take it away. She was interested. I had just learned how to use music and prayer to quiet my soul and practice God's presence. So we started to take time in the morning on the ride to school to listen to some music and be quiet afterward to let God bring his peace to her heart and body. She memorized verses like "Be still, and know that I am God" (Ps 46:10) and turned to God whenever panic came. And even though she still got nervous, she was able to get through it.

Now she knows how to have short retreats with God during the day, and to start her day in silence and quiet, giving God space in her life. She learned that problems often aren't dealt with by eliminating them, but they are opportunities for our formation and drawing near to God, things we might not learn if the problems had never been there in the first place.

One of my practices has been to read the psalms over and over. As I read them, I noted that the main themes are the kingdom of God and how that rule of life was God's dream for the world. And it had a refrain that I heard repeatedly, that God cared for and acted on behalf of the poor, the oppressed, the fatherless, the orphaned, the widow and the alien, those who are overlooked and vulnerable. I had heard the cry of my son, my wife and my daughter. Were there others right in front of me that I was missing? I asked God to help me to see the overlooked and to hear the unheard cries. I began to notice the gang-related activities listed in the newspaper and started to pray for gang members and the area of town rife with violence and life was hard. Though I had never been to that part of town, I began to make friends with leaders from that area. Soon God directed me to others with the same concern. The result: our church helped plant a multiethnic church in the area and partnered with others in creating a community development organization to provide tutoring, clothing and job training services.

I also noticed that I didn't have many friendships with those outside the bubble of my church life and ministry relationships.

But as I opened up to my family, I became available to my wife's and kids' friends. Cheri, for example, had a friend whose first-grade son, Joel, had found his father dead one morning while mom was out of town. The trauma created new problems. He was acting out at school and unable to be with or talk to adults, especially males. Unplanned, we met the family at the airport while traveling to Florida. I invited Joel, his sister and mother with us into the airline VIP lounge. Having just heard Joel's story, I asked him to sit with me apart from the others. Joel didn't say much. Suddenly I had an idea. I asked him if he would like to go to a Minnesota Twins game and sit behind home plate with a friend of mine, a former reliever for the Twins. We would get to eat with the team and meet all of Joel's favorite players. He liked the idea.

That game allowed me to break through to Joel. He began to open up to me and soon was out of his shell. When we got together, he initiated conversation. Over the next few years I took him out every once and a while. It really didn't amount to much: we'd golf, play guitars or just eat out a few times a year. His mother said she had seen him change. He was more open to males and doing better in school. He eventually asked me to be with him at his confirmation at another church in town, and I gave him a Bible devotional. Joel is now a very talented student, and we occasionally see each other.

One day in prayer I realized that God had answered my prayers to see those he saw, people I overlooked due to being so preoccupied with professional "ministry." And even though some of them were in places I might have expected, in less desirable areas of our city, I realized that orphans, widows and the oppressed are all around us. Stopping and becoming more available to my family had introduced me to a whole world of opportunity that I was missing. My friend Susan Phillips is right:

friendship is the most undervalued practice in view of its formational effect. Relationships are the context for transformation. When Jesus came to the end of his three-year association with his disciples, he was no longer just a master teacher with disciples but was their friend (Jn 15:15). To be close to Jesus is to learn the art of relationships and friendship.

No One Closer to the Spirit of Christ

C. S. Lewis said of George MacDonald, a writer and preacher of the nineteenth century, that there was no one he knew who was closer to the Spirit of Christ. MacDonald knew the power of relationships and what they could teach us about formation. Besides his fantasy stories, which Lewis was first captured by, he wrote many novels about the lessons family, friends and ordinary people could learn by inviting Christ into their everyday interactions. The books are more than just stories, they teach and deliver pithy sermons through MacDonald's characters.

MacDonald grew up in a very stern and Calvinistic Christianity, the kind that believed God created the majority of humans just to destroy them eternally. Because MacDonald didn't teach or preach that kind of Christianity, he was considered a renegade and forced out of his first church. He saw God as a loving Father, not as a distant and angry Judge. And MacDonald's novels illustrate his theology.

In *Donal Grant,* for instance, a woman plagued by her fear of God's wrath comes to see God through Jesus: "she could now think of Him as at the root of every delight in the world . . . think of Him as altogether loving and true, the veritable Father of Jesus Christ, as like could be like, more like him than any one other in the universe could be like." And in *Salted with Fire,* a minister explains to a troubled parishioner with problems approaching God: "It can only be because we do not yet see God

as He is—and that must be because we do not yet really understand Jesus—do not see the glory of God in His face. God is just
like Him."

MacDonald had problems with theories of the atonement
that view God as part loving and part wrathful, never allowing
us to know how we stand with him and making us to look only
at the cross instead of also seeking the heart of the triune God
to find his love for us. But MacDonald's faith was no soft-and-
easy liberal moralism. He saw that God's great heart of love
called for us to love as greatly, and his theme was obedience,
simple and without hesitation, evidenced in the smallest of ob-
ligations met.

While the Calvinism of his day turned out Christians concerned with correct beliefs and a list of dos and don'ts, Mac-
Donald saw God's solution to sin as making the sinner "unwill-
ing to sin again." When a person entered into the rigorous but
loving discipleship of Jesus, they would, bit by bit, shed the shell
of the old self in an exacting school of obedience. This would
cause the person to be supernaturally renewed to desire and
taste the goodness of God's way, losing taste for anything less.
And as his stories showed, this school was the everyday life of
family and friends at home, school, work and play.

My experience has confirmed MacDonald's homegrown discipleship and Lewis's testimony of being surprised by the joy of
what God can do in our lives right at home with our loved ones.
MacDonald confirms my experience for formation by family
and friends in his novel *What's Mine's Mine:* "The reward of
parents who have tried to be good, may be to learn with a joy-
ous humility, from their children."

THOMAS TRAHERNE'S CENTURIES OF MEDITATIONS
Besides George MacDonald, a writer who greatly influenced

C. S. Lewis is seventeenth-century writer Thomas Traherne. He was virtually unrecognized until the twentieth century, his writings being found hidden away and forgotten, with one piece actually saved from a fire, the pages blackened and ashen. Traherne writes of how our world is full of God's glory and that humans are temples of that glory. If we would realize how glorious we are, how interacting with each other is a direct contact with heaven and God, we would never treat each other so lightly and callously. Traherne writes about having a vision of the world as the Father's palace, and ordinary people as his habitations and temples:

> Your enjoyment of the world is never right, till every morning you awake in Heaven: see yourself in your Father's palace: and look upon the skies and the earth and the air as celestial joys. . . .
>
> You enjoyment is never right, till you esteem every Soul so great a treasure as our Savior doth.

Traherne wrote: "so eye the Lord and become a mirror, home and temple of God," which I try to practice so others might get a good eyeful of their Father in me and see God. Formation that is only about theology, practices or even spiritualities, and not people, is without the Father's heart. The best saints I know aren't pastors, writers, speakers or professional Christian workers. They are ordinary mothers and fathers who love not just their own kids but those ignored by their neighbors. They are blue-collar workers who fix the widow's car or use vacation time to work with organizations like Habitat for Humanity. They are teachers with little pay who minister unnoticed in the inner city. They are the obscure millionaires who not only fund but also bear the burden as board members of kingdom-sized endeavors in countries closed to the gospel. These are the salt and light of the world.

Their work might never be in the spotlight or receive any earthly glory. But they and their work will not go unnoticed or unrewarded. Like Traherne's writings, which he thought he was only writing for himself, God and a few others, someday God will pluck them out of obscurity and they and their works will shine like the sun before the very angels of heaven.

Let Me So Eye Thee

Oh let me so eye thee till I turn into thee
And look upon me till Thou art found in me
That I may be a mirror of thy brightness,
An habitation of thy love
And a temple of thy glory.
—Thomas Traherne

6

Church as a Catching Force

W*hat does it look like when a whole church, not just one ministry position or one department, enters into intentional Christian spiritual formation? Could following Jesus as a community be a force that catches others up into God's kingdom?*

After several years of intentionally reorganizing our church toward making and becoming disciples of Jesus, we becan to see some remarkable changes. The call came to one of our Open Door pastors. A couple was asking if they could schedule a dedication service for their child. Normally requests for dedications don't need top management approval. But this one did. Paul, the pastor responsible for dedications, explained to us that everything was going as usual until he took the parents' names to send them more information. Paul noticed that both parents were female, and after an awkward pause the caller said, "Oh. by the way, we are lesbians. Will that be a problem? And oh yeah, our child is African American, we're white."

After explaining to the caller the church's views on same-sex relationships, Paul found that the mother and her partner were well aware of the church's stand on the matter. And they were still very interested in having their child dedicated. Paul asked,

"So, given our views, why would you want to have your child dedicated at Open Door?" Her answer presented us with a surprisingly wonderful dilemma. "We know the church's position on our partnership, but we have felt so welcome and loved here, much more than any other church, even the gay/lesbian/transsexual church we used to attend, that we wanted our child to be raised in this church, where he would experience what we have. We feel safe here, we feel God's presence here. We know you may not be able to do it, but wanted to know if something was possible."

After some good debate within our team (wouldn't Jesus welcome this little one to himself?), we decided to do a creative reworking of how we normally dedicate children, one that would bless everything we possibly could. Paul put together a private service we would do in their home, and we began a conversation on what family is all about in God's kingdom.

CAUGHT UP INTO THE KINGDOM

As I ministered in my church, I found that my team wasn't always sure how to respond to those who were attracted to our church and how to minister to the variety of needs. However, I was grateful to see the "catching force" at work as God's kingdom manifested itself among the leaders and attendees. Without using any of the usual marketing strategies, I discovered that we could attract those who wouldn't normally go to church. We were just being ourselves and pursuing the kingdom as we see it in Jesus.

That kind of atmosphere isn't manufactured by having parking-lot greeters and newcomer kiosks in the foyer (though these can be useful). It is the result of the gospel of the kingdom pervading the life and message of a church community, large or small. As I work with various pastors and churches, I find that when the life-changing gospel is preached and lived out in example, though we aren't perfect, others are caught up in the life of the kingdom of God. As we enter into it, others just follow after us.

Most of what is powerful in our life, whether good or bad, is caught, almost by osmosis, in non-orchestrated life-on-life interactions. And when we intentionally move into God's kingdom life, our ministry supernaturally becomes like the contagious life of Jesus. Just as people did anything they could to get next to Jesus, the gates of hell can't stop people from forcing their way into our ministry.

A church with this kind of life becomes a "catching force," and its staff and members don't have to do much more than be who they are to grow and affect the culture. Maybe the sign of how much the gospel is missing in our churches is how hard we have to try to make our organizations attractive through programming rather than with our compelling lives in community with God.

But both demonstration and proclamation of the gospel are equally necessary. And a compelling gospel demonstration is dependent on a clear and powerful proclamation of the good news—it has the power to evoke life change by God's Spirit. When proclamation is backed up by a consistent demonstration of those who are becoming "good news," it is the most effective program for the church. I find that when an individual, pastor or church discovers the gospel of the kingdom, a fire starts that spreads quickly with remarkable power.

PROCLAIMING THE GOSPEL

Apart from being an example ourself, the most important thing we can do to lead a church, organization or group into whole life transformation is to study Scripture to see what life looks like in the kingdom and begin to preach, teach and proclaim it. I'm not talking about one or two preaching or teaching series on spiritual formation or the kingdom. Everything we teach and preach must be reimagined in light of life in the kingdom. Then God shows up in some startling ways, and we don't have to do anything more to draw people in than present the good news. When we focus on Jesus and the promise of his life, powerful works of God's Spirit show up without having to prime the pump.

One of our pastors presented a sermon series on the Ten Commandments, which he had framed as wedding vows that God had made with Israel. He related these vows to Jesus' Sermon on the Mount, noting that Jesus was the new Moses and that we could also leave our slavery to sin for a life in loving obedience by following him. He reminded our people that Jesus was not a "Christian" but God chose to send his Son as a Torah-observant Jew and a rabbi or teacher who proclaimed God's kingdom. This series has had some remarkable consequences in our church. Each of the commandments came to life as ways to live in love with God and others. And in this kind of new life, people of all kinds have been drawn in, just as people were when Jesus preached.

Nadia, who had come to church at the invitation of a friend, approached one of the pastors after the service and ask for advice. She explained that she was Jewish but wanted to know whether she could become a follower of Jesus without becoming a Christian.

Without hesitating he replied, "Yes, of course." (The earliest followers of Jesus didn't call themselves Christians—they and others referred to the movement as a fulfillment of the Hebrew faith, a "sect of the Jews" or "followers of the Way." See Paul's words in Acts 24:14.)

A bit startled and apparently expecting to be turned down or at least met with some resistance, she protested, "Don't you want to know why?"

It seems that Nadia's family still told stories of relatives who were prisoners in German concentration camps. They remembered "Christian" guards' cross necklaces swaying to and fro as they mocked, abused, beat and killed the prisoners. She also explained that her husband would not be happy with her new adventure in life, but the invitation to live the way of this rabbi was what her heart longed for.

A few weeks later Nadia reported to the pastor that her kids were confused by her playing CDs of the pastor's sermons about Jesus in the car. And her husband was quite unsettled and disturbed with all of this. But he respected his wife and began to pray to his Adonai for clarity and wisdom on how to respond to his wife's interest in the rabbi Jesus. Then he had a dream that puzzled him: his wife appeared to him in a blue dress, holding a book in one hand and a lamb in the other. He got the meaning of the blue dress, it was the color of the flag of Israel, and the book was the Torah.

The dream seemed to be a confirmation that Nadia's disturbing new way of life was not far from the ideals of Judaism. "But what is the lamb all about?" he asked her.

From her knowledge of the Hebrew Scriptures and the teaching of the Gospels about Jesus, she explained that the lamb pointed to the Passover sacrifices, which were fulfilled in rabbi Jesus and his exodus from death into new life. Nadia and her family still don't call themselves Christians, and they may never identify culturally with Christianity, but Jesus has entered their lives.

A church that clearly defines what it means to follow Jesus into the kingdom of God becomes a catching force. Nadia illustrates what happens when a church abandons the reduced gospel and embraces whole life transformation.

Sometimes those raised with a reduced gospel are disturbed when a church doesn't have traditional altar calls to "accept Jesus as your personal Savior." For them, the call to consistently follow Jesus and embrace life in the kingdom is not the gospel. When I explain that accepting Jesus as personal Savior but not necessarily Lord makes discipleship optional, they don't seem to understand. They think the alternative is to embrace some version of the Social Gospel, which amounts to works righteousness. Calling people to the saving life of Jesus and to life under his power as Lord is embracing all aspects of salvation. Jesus is not just interested in heaven but also our whole life and social situation.

Nadia's journey included learning what it means to love her enemies. When a staff member told of his experience with Jordanian Muslims who were finding Jesus but not taking on the cultural trappings of Western Christianity, Nadia came up to the podium quite agitated. She asked how she could ever come to embrace a Muslim, asking, "Aren't they our enemies?"

We explained that Jesus' followers come from all kinds of religious, political, socioeconomic and ethnic backgrounds.

During the 2004 U.S. presidential election, Church of the Open Door received a complaint from an attendee because she saw several bumper stickers for Democratic candidate John Kerry in the parking lot. She presumed our church was on the "right" (red) side of the political spectrum. After a few weeks she wrote us to apologize. Through the preaching she began to understand that Christians aren't red or blue, but are for the poor, the rich and all who need God's kingdom rule in their lives.

On another occasion our leadership team found out that a Mormon missionary stationed in Minneapolis had been invited by a friend to attend our services. He knew the differences between the Mormon and evangelical faith and came to spread the Mormon version. But as he heard the gospel explained as a radically different kind of life, not just doctrinal beliefs to be accepted, he was drawn to follow Jesus. This created crisis at his Mormon school, where he was given a full ride as one of the rising stars in the athletic program. What had happened in his life was not a matter of doctrinal beliefs that could be easily left behind. He had found a new kind of life—and that now made him dangerous.

BEGINNING WITH THE LEADERS

Becoming a church focused on spiritual formation involves centering everything—our individual and corporate lives, our teaching and preaching, our children's programming, even the songs we sing—on the kingdom. But before we retool the church mission and vision statements or programs, it starts with the leaders. Transformation begins in our lives, our relationships with each other and our families. When we enter into whole life transformation, at first nothing in the church changes except for us. We begin by understanding and living the gospel.

So our teaching and pastoral teams began studying the gospel of the kingdom in the Scriptures, aided by the teachings of Dallas Willard, N. T. Wright, Scot McKnight, Jean Vanier and others. Before trying to teach what we were learning, we first had to practice these truths in our daily relationships. We did not want to get ahead of what we were actually experiencing. This is called the discipline of secrecy. This is why I believe Jesus instructed those he healed not to tell others or to first go to the priest. Then they were to consolidate their inner and outer healing before speaking and sharing (Mt 8:4; 9:30).

In meeting with a local church that wanted to move into spiritual formation, I explained that this is not primarily a Bible study or a one-to-two-year program but more like learning a language. It takes time and means becoming immersed in a different way of living. We were trying to move into it more organically than programmatically or organizationally. (Both are necessary, but one is prior to and must not be lost to the other.) One person finally got what I was trying to say, and asked, "If we get .01 percent of our people into this in the next year, we would be doing good, right?" I said, "You got it! And the .01 percent would be you—this committee or group of leaders—living it out together in your homes, neighborhoods and work."

Our language about salvation did change, but not in the use of spiritual-formation terms. If we used the technical words and contemplative terms presented at spiritual formation conferences, we would lose the average hearer. Along with salvation being seen as following Jesus as Master or Lord, and not just Savior, we also began to unpack the word *transformation,* the gradual change God does in cooperation with us and in community. But we didn't do this with classes that defined and spelled out "Christian spiritual formation." We teach on the three passages that use words associated with *formation:* Galatians 4:19 (formed), Romans 8:29 (conformed), and 2 Corinthians 3:18 (transformed). This is as far as we go in using technical spiritual formation language. Most of our teaching is about how life looks in the kingdom of God.

And we don't refer a lot to ancient practices, various spiritualities (e.g., Celtic or Ignatian) or saints—although we are familiar with these and make them our own. We proclaim what it means to (1) live free of contempt, worry and lust as found in the Sermon on the Mount, (2) cultivate the fruit of the Spirit and (3) repent by putting on Christ's new life and putting off our old one. We urge what one writer has called "naked intent"—plain, old willingness to obey and learn by signing up as a student or apprentice to Jesus and using all means to practice Christ's life. N. T. Wright says that to have Jesus as Lord means Jesus is "making all things right." This is our way of talking about the effects of justification in both its declarative and substantive nature.

I teach a class on Christian character and the disciplines, but I call it "The Good Life and How to Get There," joking that the *discipline* sounds like someone is going to get a spanking. We also use the ancient practice *lectio divina* and its modern adaptation, centering prayer, which are prayers of quiet or contemplation. But we carefully teach the background to this kind of prayer, explaining that like David, who "stilled and quieted [his] soul; / like a weaned child with its mother" (Ps 131:2; see also Ps 37; 46), we are being still and experiencing God's presence without words, thoughts or images.

I was on a plane waiting to take off when the pilot said we would be delayed for a few minutes due to some technical issues. While we waited, we could accidentally hear the chatter between pilot and the engineers repairing whatever had gone wrong: "The hydraulic line obstruction in the second section facility is being overhauled and redirected and we should be functional in about ten minutes." When the problem was fixed and we were about to taxi to the runway, the pilot came back on and in layperson's terms said, "The toilets were stopped up and we had to blow out the lines—everything is good now, so we are ready to take off." Teaching about being transformed into Christ's life doesn't need to be technical or hard to understand, even though it is difficult to put into practice. In fact such talk might be a sign of resistance to real discipleship. But it doesn't need to be made more difficult by using language that obscures it. Doing so just might betray our proclivity toward a double life or remaking spiritual formation into useless head knowledge and lifeless applications or practices.

Most often we talk about being able to love an enemy, being a good and faithful friend of Jesus and others, finding liberty from addictions and freedom to partner with God, serving others in tangible ways for Christ's kingdom, especially the least and the poor (modern equivalents of the alien, orphaned, widowed, oppressed and vulnerable). People are challenged with the vision of a kingdom-sized life and community expression in marriage, friendship, church committees and task groups. Then spiritual formation gets as practical as not gossiping, being direct in speech, and fighting well in love rather living in unreconciled and fractured alliances.

"Practicing the Presence" Evangelism

At Open Door as we took time to rethink, revision, repurpose and retool our whole church into transformational life, we changed some things and made them public, encouraging people to participate. We had been a "recovery" church, and now with formation being our emphasis it was leading us to reach out in a new way. We announced in a sermon our new outreach program but noted it would not entail people coming to church any more than they already were for "outreach programming" and really didn't ask them do anything different in their normal activities. We taught "practicing the presence of Jesus" in our everyday lives and experienced it corporately in our worship services. This means we are doing things with Jesus rather than just for him, consciously acting with Jesus and his Spirit. Practicing the presence of Jesus in our everyday lives, he said, is helping people see Jesus as we look to him and them.

We explained that when we are talking with someone and we look at something beyond or behind the person while still talking with him or her, the person will notice and look that way too.

If we are learning how to live in Jesus' presence consciously more and more each day in more of the moments of our lives, we will be unconsciously looking to Jesus in everything we do. And others will begin to see him too. They will see who the eyes of our hearts see, where our gaze is fixed upon—Jesus. He will reveal himself in us, his living Bibles.

This teaching was enhanced by a series titled "The Locker Room," which introduced our core values. This called our people to see ministry as being primarily their everyday lives and only secondarily as the church's weekend events or activities.

A postal worker took this seriously and began to pray for those on his route as he delivered the mail. He practiced Jesus' presence and followed his lead each moment without doing harm to his job or becoming an obnoxious witness, just a gentle and intentional force for good wherever he went. This is what Todd Hunter calls "being the cooperative friends of Jesus seeking to live constant lives of creative goodness, through the power of the Holy Spirit, for the sake of others." The mail carrier took enough interest in others that he soon found himself in short conversations and eventually was praying with people on the route—he even helped in the wedding of one and baptism of another.

Evangelistic programs and techniques for sharing the gospel will never take the place of giving someone a new way to live with God. Techniques and shortcut tricks often betray a basically godless and relationally stunted life. People need a powerful and life-transforming experience with the living Jesus, like that of the blind man in John 9, who said, in effect, "All I know is that I once was blind, but now I see. And the one who did this for me and is now with me is Jesus." And his words would be backed up with the undeniable and unmistakable reality of a changed and contagious life that is caught, not taught.

In this way we started to reimagine everything in the corporate life and ministry of the Church of the Open Door.

UNCOMFORTABLE WORSHIP

Before the last of three services at our church, a guest speaker commented to me, "There is something different about how you do worship. It is formational, but I can't tell you quite how—I just know it is. And yet not in a heavily themed way with 'spiritual formation' slogans on the walls." The preparation, prayer time, songs and leaders were obviously doing everything with formation as their goal, but it was done in more of a spirit than with some programmatic and artificial spiritual-formation spin. If there is any programmatic intention, it is to help people live into the truth in worship and word in such a way as to bring them from where they are to where they should be. Formation is more about calling people to experience change in their attitudes and then their behaviors than it is learning how to define *spiritual formation.* And that often means messing with our comfort zones where we are molded by the world and need to be re-formed by God.

One Open Door service was about being loved by Christ and its corollary, loving our enemy. After each service prayer ministers usually stand in the front. This time we had them in the foyer, where people were exiting the service. The reason was that we had a seven-foot high cross in front, decorated with pictures of all kinds of people: unknown Iraqi and U.S. soldiers, celebrities like Pat Robertson and Madonna, politicians like George Bush and Hilary Clinton, laborers and professionals, and the aged and newborn of many ethnicities. The intention was to represent everyone God loves but we sometimes hate. Scriptures about loving enemies, blessing those who curse us, considering others better than ourselves, not judging lest we be judged and showing mercy to the merciless were read aloud. Songs like Francis's prayer, "Lord make me an instrument of thy peace," were sung.

There were many who couldn't take it. Some had to leave the room in their repulsion to loving someone too far to the left or right of them politically or culturally. Our prayer ministers reported amazing interactions, helping people face their prejudices and confessing their lack of love. Some were overcome by their own sense of not being loved. This was a way of not only communicating our vision and values about whole life transformation but actually helping people enter into formational realities with their whole being, not just their minds.

Another example is how we conduct communion. We teach more by what we do and how we do things than by what we say about those actions. Prior to receiving the communion elements, we were confessing our sins alone in our seats with our eyes closed, and most of our sins didn't involve more than God and our individual self, so we needed to bring communal aspects to this practice. After studying formation and the nature of communion, we changed from the common evangelical practice of passing trays of bread and cups to seated people who serve themselves. The cross, we began to see, reconciles people in community, who subsequently serve Christ by serving each other with his gifts. Our old way of doing communion didn't express that and actually reinforced the aspects we wanted to transform, that of a very privatized gospel, just about Jesus and me, not others.

We felt that communion helps us to experience God individually and corporately. In fact, as the Eastern Orthodox say, Eucharist creates church, the one body of Christ. So we adopted the ancient style of worshipers proceeding down the church aisles to sets of two servers, one serving the bread and another the cup. The servers are trained to look each communicant in the eye, place the bread in their hand, say a blessing over them that incorporates that day's message about being whole (e.g., "this is Christ's body broken for your wholeness" and "this cup is your healing in his blood"). It is wonderful to see whole families, friends and couples taking communion before the servers as little flocks of Jesus.

Another example of how everyday worship was the transforming people is how they handled their money. As part of a series on money, sex and power, our people were invited to consecrate each of these in a special service that capped the teaching on each one. At the money consecration we read corporate prayers affirming the teaching we received and renouncing money as an idol and service to mammon, confessing our sins of indebtedness and greed, and requesting healing from disordered financial habits and for generous giving and blessings for financial freedom and sacrifice for others.

A large bowl was placed at the front of the congregation, who had been prepared for this the week before. This offering was not for a church building or for making the budget, but for transformation of lives conformed to the idols of materialism. There was weeping and crying during songs of worship as people processed at will to place money, clipped credit cards and business cards in the bowl as symbols of God's new ownership. Gold and silver watches and jewelry, even Starbucks coffee mugs and house keys were likewise placed in the bowl, symbolizing decisions to not go ahead with purchases or to embrace a more simplified lifestyle.

In a series titled "The Ten Commandments of Giving," a second offering was taken without any idea of who would receive it, a truly generous offering given to God first. The amount came to over half of our regular general-fund weekly offering. In the plate were checks, bills, coins and even pieces of lint, evidence that people were literally emptying their pockets in hilarious giving to God alone. Along with a couple of staff, it was my privilege to bless various organizations with large checks that they hadn't expected. We are amazed at God's release of the grip of mammon on our people. We have come to see giving as a transformational activity that is more than just giving to and supporting the church. Giving is a way of life and loosing our grip on money must be accompanied by the same with our time, passions and the rest of our lives.

WILL REVIVAL COME?

The best formation "program" to make disciples in a church is for the pastor, staff and top lay leaders to serve as models of transformation. Then the catching force begins to operate and we see it imitated in the body.

We have all seen churches get caught up in a "sin storm" of gossip, slander and division. But the opposite is also possible: a church caught up in a wave of love and repentance bringing unity and witness. A truly transformed church is the best program of evangelism. Is such revival possible today?

In her book *The Great Emergence,* Phyllis Tickle makes the case that we are living in a another great reforming time, a hinge in history, culture and religion like the Protestant Reformation of the 1500s and the awakenings of the last two centuries. She sees a whirlwind of forces from the four corners of American Christianity—the Penecostal-renewalists, mainline liturgicals, traditional evangelical-conservatives, and social justice Christians—mixing into something that will bring forth a new expression of the church. She believes this happens every five hundred years and is a way of the church "cleaning out the attic" and renewing itself. The church that rises from the older form has the effect of spreading Christianity more than ever before.

I hope she is right. But the key to revival or reform is not innovative methods or theology, but recovery of basic obedience to Jesus and recovery of classic discipleship for a living faith. As we have seen in the nineteenth century, discipleship as doctrinal head knowledge or outward behavior results in the double life (see chapter two). And in the *Oxford Handbook of Evangeli-*

cal Theology, Dallas Willard writes that for evangelicals since World War II, "there has simply been no consistent general teaching or practice under the heading of discipleship among evangelicals of this period: none that would be recognizable *as* discipleship in terms of biblical teaching or of the Christian past." Willard argues that any powerful discipleship has the rabbinic element Jesus had with his disciples, being together in everyday life.

As Jesus traveled, he did three things in the synagogues, homes and public areas: he *announced* the availability of life in the kingdom of God, he *taught* how things were done in the kingdom of God, and he *manifested* the present power of the kingdom through amazing deeds (Mt 4:23; 9:35; Lk 4:18-44). Then, after a period of training, he sent his disciples to do the things they had heard and seen him do—continuing all the while to evaluate their work and to teach them as they progressed. This continued through his life, trial and death, and during his postresurrection presence with them. His instruction as he left was for his disciples to make *disciples* of all nations—of all types of people—and he promised he would be *with them* always until the end of the age (Mt 28:19-20).

If Phyllis Tickle is right and we are in a time of reform, it is this kind of life that must be recovered in our communities and churches, families and friendships. Tickle says that Protestantism in America has had no center and that perhaps a center is being formed by the centripetal forces at work in Christianity once again. If it is to hold, Christ and his life must be at the center, as Paul said, "Follow my example, as I follow the example of Christ" (1 Cor 11:1).

And that will mean getting rid of the junk in the church that gets in the way, our false imitations, our reduced gospels and the dead way of life handed down from generation to generation. Dallas Willard explains the necessary transfer of life this way:

> While the charge was to make disciples of Jesus and *not* of
> the disciples, the basic method—teaching, example, and
> imitation—remained the same as his immediate followers
> proceeded to do what he had told them to do. The method
> was: to gather a group of people by telling the story of Je-
> sus, featuring his resurrection and pending return, to show
> by example what it meant to live *with him* now, already
> beyond death, and to lead others into such a life of being
> "with Jesus, learning to be like him."

THE CATCHING FORCE AND THE NEXT GENERATION

We find that youth will stay in churches if there is a transforming message *demonstrated* by leaders showing that doing life together, including you, is possible. Then they have hope that
leadership is actually going to trust them to lead in significant
roles. We have a plan to replace our older leaders with younger
ones, and both old and young are mentoring each other as
friends. The older ones help the younger ones see what they
have seen from experience; the younger ones help their elders
see what their experience blinds them to.

As I reflect on my life, I find that this classic way of apprenticeship is how Jesus had captured me. Who I am with and the
life we share together is the most formational program I could
hope for.

In January 2008 I made a road trip with two young men to
InterVarsity's "Following Christ 2008" conference in Chicago,
where we listened to N. T. Wright, took seminar tracks with
graduate students from various disciplines (such as business
and education), worshiped, and stayed up late talking about life
and what we were hearing and experiencing. The theme was

human flourishing, and everything echoed the apostolic father Irenaeus's statement that the glory of God is humans being fully alive. I had no agenda but to be present to these two young men and do life together, being fully alive to each other and God for a few days with a little help from N. T. Wright and InterVarsity.

We were fully alive sharing stories with each other. We listened to each other's favorite tunes, the *Into the Wild* sound track by Eddie Vedder and some classic Led Zeppelin. On the way back we explored what the conference had stirred up in us. Their hearts were exploding with the truth that their formation in Christ, making them fully human, is the only way to reach their potential and subsequently would attract others to him. We explored what that meant for their life work and calling. They were excited to be mentored by me and I by them in the splash back of their fresh life in Jesus, and to be part of a new program at our church training college and graduate students to mentor junior high and high school students in intentional communities.

John Henry Newman, a convert first to evangelicalism, then to Anglicanism and finally to Roman Catholicism, was part of a movement in nineteenth-century England that tried to recover the basic teaching of the church fathers: we can flourish as humans in Christ, follow his and the saints' example, and likewise become people others could imitate into the life of Jesus. At its most powerful this life in individuals and groups would catch up others into that life. Cardinal Newman's prayer is said every day after Mass by the Missionaries of Charity, whose founder is Mother Teresa.

> Dear Jesus, help us to spread Your fragrance everywhere we go.
> Flood our souls with Your spirit and life.

Penetrate and possess our whole being so utterly that our
lives may only be a radiance of Yours.

Shine through us, and be so in us that every soul we
come in contact with may feel your presence in our
souls.

Let them look up and see no longer us, but only Jesus!

Stay with us, and then we shall shine as you shine; so to
shine as to be a light to others.

The light, O Jesus, will be all from You, none of it will be
ours; it will be You shining on others through us.

Let us preach You without preaching, not by words but
by our example, by the catching force, the sympathetic
influence of what we do, the evident fullness of the
love our hearts bear to You. Amen

Training for a
Trust That Obeys

Now that I had a vision of what obedience to Jesus could look like, how could I begin to, as the old song says, "trust and obey, for there's no other way to be happy in Jesus"? I was tired of trying harder to obey. It didn't work. Was there training available to develop my trust into habitual obedience? Who would teach me?

The man who stood before me for prayer came in response to the sermon I had just given. He was trembling with emotion. I had shared how my new understanding of whole life transformation had changed my ideas of what was possible in obeying Christ and the kind of training it required, and I was beginning to incorporate it in my life. I now trusted Christ to teach me how to obey him in areas of my life that I had little hope for change in before—areas where I had tried so many times without success and had given up. One of those areas was anger and contempt for those who did me wrong.

I now knew how I could cooperate with God's grace to train my body to actually do the things he said I could—loving my enemy and living without contempt, that disdain and ill will that kept me locked up inside. I had hope that facial expressions and sharp tongue would be rewired. Christ allows no room for grudges, hatred or even low levels of irritation with those who oppose me. Better than that, I wanted to be able to genuinely bless my enemies and even pray for their well-being. My vision was that my body would become like Teflon to anger and contempt—they wouldn't stick to me anymore and would have no hold on me. Having learned some measure of this, I knew how to offer this hope to others that they too could trust and obey in areas of life they hadn't dreamed could possibly change.

Responding to that invitation, the man came to me for prayer and didn't say anything for a bit, looking deep and longingly into my eyes with his eyes, tears streaming down his face. He was already praying with his body. Leaning toward me, his bulky frame and muscular hands communicated to me that he used his body in some kind of demanding work. He placed his hands in mine as if they were an offering. When he finally said something, he asked, "Would you pray for my hands?" He shared that he too wanted Jesus to help him to get rid of the anger that was inhabiting his heart, mind and other parts of his body.

He was now retired from the police force but shared how his job had often put him into contact with people he had termed "dirt bags." In his opinion these people were not fit to be called human. They were the wife beaters, child abusers, rapists, petty thieves, drug dealers and prostitute's clients he had encountered. He was drawn to the invitation I had made for Jesus to be not only his Savior but also Teacher. But his case was a hard one. Could he really be free of the leftover contempt and hatred that had accumulated over the years?

In praying and talking with him I affirmed that his work had been good, protecting both victim and perpetrator. But he protested that he had not known how to deal with the leftovers, which were now spilling out on his family and friends. He wanted his body to be able to respond to enemies the way Jesus had on the cross, with forgiveness and compassion, even for those he had seen as dirtbags. And he wanted to start with his hands, so that the parts of his body would become instruments for doing God's will (Rom 6:12-14).

In my sermon I had told about what God had done in my life to train me to begin to love and bless one particularly contemptuous family member who had severely hurt my wife and our family. This gave the man hope. He longed for that kind of training.

How do we train into Christlikeness? And how do we bring others along? Once we are "caught up" with a new vision of life in Jesus' kingdom and intend to do his will—to be ruled by his power—we must do more than just try harder. We must enter into training or practice, to bring our intended will into our body.

INTENDED WILL VERSUS EMBODIED WILL

Like Henry Ward Beecher's cry, this former police officer knew that "Jesus would forgive him of this sinful attitude, but would he deliver him from it too"? Would Jesus' training be powerful enough to make up for years of habitual responses to any challenge to his authority? And could he become proficient at being good so that his body would respond with easy and unforced obedience as his most natural response? Could his good intentions actually become a reality in his body?

I first heard of this possibility from Dallas Willard, who explained that our *intended will,* our thoughts and desires to act as Jesus says we should, needs to become our *embodied will.* That is, our intended will is incarnated through training, resulting in new habits of mouth, hands, eyes and body. Dallas applied this to ordinary road rage, the kind we all experience and participate in. When we are confronted with an angry and rude driver, our knee-jerk response of cursing them under our breath is due to a habit we developed in the course of our life, first having heard our parents or a friend do so and then over time we make it our own, becoming an easy and reflexive response. And by God's grace and power these habits can be put to death and new ones brought to life. Our knee-jerk reaction to rude people will become one of automatic blessing.

If we partner with Jesus and his supernatural power and train for change, cursing others will become a distant memory as we naturally bless them, hoping things will turn out well for them. Of course we could try to do this without Jesus. But we would be pumping out a behavior without a heart change. We may do it as a way to prove ourself better than the other, but then we would not truly be transformed.

On the cross, Jesus' embodied reaction to the cursings, jeers and taunts of the two thieves, the religious leaders, and Roman soldiers was to bless them and pray for God to forgive them. He didn't have to think about it or push back anger and contempt. His supernaturally natural response was to bless. With small steps and victories along the way, Jesus had trained all his life for this moment.

The early disciple Stephen had entered into Jesus' school and trained to put up with abuse from people like Saul of Tarsus, who along with others stoned him. Stephen's blessing was not some staged or forced imitation of Jesus for the jeering crowd. It had become his supernaturally natural response.

And the proof that these responses weren't staged or forced is in the reaction from those who observed them. One thief repented and asked to go wherever Jesus was going (or at least to remember him when there; Lk 23:42-43), and a Roman soldier came to believe that the charge against Jesus was really true, he was some kind of God to act like that (Lk 23:47)! After witnessing Stephen's forgiving face and his prayer, "Lord, do not hold this sin against them" (Acts 7:60), Saul was won over by Jesus' severe mercy to him on the road to Damascus (Acts 9:4-5). Later, as Paul, he would urge us to present our bodies as living sacrifices, which is true worship (Rom 12:1-2), which would be evidenced by blessing others when cursed (Rom 12:14).

GOLF SWINGS AND OBEDIENCE

At the conference where I first heard this, Dallas went on to explain how we could develop such supernaturally natural and easy responses. He explained that this kind of embodied willful action only comes about by a deliberate and protracted practice or training. Upon hearing Dallas explain this, a conference participant who is a personal friend of the professional golfer Tom Lehman leaned over to me. Hardly able to contain his excitement, he said, "That's what Tom says about his golf swing when he is in the groove and has practiced well—he doesn't even think about his swing, how he grips the club, eye on the ball, shoulder down, just like all the instructors tell beginning and advanced golfers—none of that is in his mind, it just is what comes out of his body without even thinking!"

But Tom Lehman didn't just watch a golf video and then play in tournaments that way. He had to train and practice, progressing bit by bit until what was a concentrated effort became his seemingly unconscious response. Too often Christians jump from trusting Jesus for forgiveness and power over sin to a frustrating attempt at trying to obey that fails time and again due to a lack of training. We can't stop cursing our enemies by "trying" without learning and practicing new behaviors under the guidance of the Spirit. And character is not something we can produce by ourself in our own sinful flesh. We need God's mysterious training through which he puts to death our old habits and brings to life new ones, and we respond with our best efforts.

Second Peter says we must "make every effort" to enable God to do in us what is impossible without him—it's a divine and human synergy and cooperation (2 Pet 1:3-9).

TRYING HARDER VERSUS TRAINING THAT WORKS

Training for life is just like training for anything else. If we try to do something that requires a degree of difficulty or meaning, we will need to set aside time to practice. We can't try once or twice, even with great effort, and expect to get the same result as we would with careful and long-term training. This was illustrated for me in a very trying experience I had driving a car. I had agreed to take a friend in his car to the airport. We had a good talk for the half hour it took to get there while he drove. Once there, he took his bags and was about to leave for the security line when I called out in a frantic plea, "Tom, come back here, man! We have a big problem!" I hadn't noticed that his car was a stick shift, which I didn't know how to use. So here I was, with a friend's car that I couldn't drive, in a busy airport.

So, I asked him what we should do, hoping he would say let's go to a "park and fly" nearby and you can call for a ride. But after quick instructions on how to shift, he smiled and said, "Go ahead and try. You can do it! See yah." And off he went into the airport to catch his plane. So I did try. With just the little head knowledge I had about clutches and shifting, and with lots of fear (I have test anxiety anyway) I put in the clutch and, lurching and stalling a number of times, finally made it onto the ramp to the highway, going just fast enough in the right lane while sweating profusely.

But then I panicked when I realized that I might have to slow down. *Don't you have to downshift these things to go slower? I will strip the gears just braking!* With my knee on the wheel, I grabbed the car manual from the glove compartment and paged through it, but I didn't find anything on downshifting. When I did slow down, my worst fears didn't occur. And I finally landed his in the driveway, exhausted. I never want to try that again or to have that kind of a training experience again. I did finally learn, but in a parking lot, where I could practice by trial and error and perfect my use of a stick shift in a relaxed manner.

This is an example of trying without training. Athletes who do not go to training camp have difficulty making the team or don't perform well during the season. Christians who don't follow Jesus into training can't perform well either. Without ever seeing any real progress, many have thereby given up on obedience. But once they see the wisdom of training and cooperate with God's gracious enabling, a whole new world of possibilities appears and the life pictured in Scripture comes alive.

WALKING ON WATER

"Virtue Walk" is one of the training exercises I have developed to cooperate with Jesus for specific life change. It began in my own life as I, like Peter, tried to "walk on water" or have power over areas of my life. It is based on 2 Peter 1:1-10, which tells us that in Jesus we have all we need to participate in life and godliness, and can escape the corruption found in our culture.

> For this very reason, make every effort to add to your faith goodness; and to goodness, knowledge; and to knowledge, self control; and to self control, perseverance; and to perseverance, godliness; and to godliness, mutual affection; and to mutual affection, love. For if you possess these qualities in increasing measure, they will keep you from being ineffective and unproductive in your knowledge of our Lord Jesus Christ. But if any of you do not have them, you are nearsighted and blind, and you have forgotten that

you have been cleansed from your past sins. (vv. 5-9 TNIV)

The passage says that our cleansing from sin has the added benefit of power over sin and a good and virtuous life. Verses 10-11 say that we are to make every effort to do these things and we will not stumble, becoming productive and effective in loving others, even enemies, like Jesus. Those who live like this will find a "rich welcome" in the kingdom.

The "Virtue Walk" develops a picture of transformation in specific areas of my life, and requires careful training plans to accomplish it. First I need to envision what *goodness* would look like in particular areas of my life.

Money: If I were out of control in spending and full of greed, what would it be like to be content and free to be generous with what I have?

Sex: If I were a slave to lust, what would it look like to be uninterested in lustful fantasies and to be intimate with others without lust?

Prayerfulness: If I were to go through my day without much of God's presence and partnering, what would it look like to know his voice, to sense his mind on things, to know that he is with me—like a best friend sitting beside me and ready to engage me at a moment's notice?

Anger or control: If I were angry and controlling, what would it look like to be able to put away anger quickly and to trust others and God for outcomes rather than manipulate things or people to accomplish my idea of what is best?

Fear or worry: If I were living in fear or worried about some matter, what would it be like to be able to trust God's provision for that area and be peaceful, no matter what was happening?

I broke the Virtue Walk down into the various components, identifying a recurring thought, feeling, attitude, behavior or habit of sin to be transformed. Besides having a clear vision of a good outcome in my life, I would also need to develop a strong intention or willingness to obey or at least to admit my lack of intention and ask for God to help me intend what he wanted for me.

Then I developed an actual plan of practices and training exercises to do in that specific area of life. This involved finding the appropriate spiritual disciplines that would put me in a place where God could rewire my internal and external life. As an apprentice of Jesus the training in these disciplines reformed the reactions and habits of particular parts of my body. With lots of trial and error, all smothered in God's grace and mercy, I expected Jesus to bring some real and tangible goodness to my life—but in his time and in his way.

MY TRAINING FOR WORRY: CARE CASTING

One particular practice that I developed to eliminate worry is "care casting." My worry has decreased and has been replaced with patience and rest when circumstances don't go my way. There are still aspects of my wiring for worry that set me to fretting, but I also know how to recover from this and find peace by what I call "care casting." I take seriously the verses "Do not be anxious about anything" (Phil 4:6) and "casting all your care upon him" (1 Pet 5:7 KJV), finding peace in obediently trusting God's care for me, which guards my heart and mind.

If there is something that concerns me, I just keep on giving it to Jesus in prayer and have learned to keep from taking it back into my consciousness. When it does show up, I just give it back up to God. After a while I actually lose the worry to God, and he keeps it from harassing me. I catch his peace in the process by continually being present to God rather than to my worry or fear. When I guard myself against my cares, I replace the presence of worry with Jesus himself, and in the process I am caught up in his peace.

My son loves to fish, and he always reminds me when we are bass fishing that the lure has to be in the water to catch fish. The fish won't find the lure if it is in the boat. I also have found that to catch peace I need to keep casting my concerns and requests, my cares, into God's hands.

The remarkable thing about these exercises is that when we work on one area of our life, say worry or contempt, it has incredible crossover effects on other areas. Working on one area brings our whole body into a process of training for obedience. I intended to act differently in one area and asked God to work my intention into my body for every area. Romans 12:1-2 became a prayer for me.

> I offer my body to you, Jesus, as a living sacrifice. Set it apart from worry, anger, rage and contempt, and make it acceptable to you. This only makes sense in view of how you have poured yourself out on me with mercy after mercy. Let me not be molded any longer by the world, but transform me totally by changing the way I think and feel about everything in my life. Make me living proof of your kingdom life in my very body.

The Virtue Walk can apply to all Christians.

There is no greater reward in proclaiming the good news of life in Jesus than seeing people begin to realize that they can actually become good. And when they do, I find that many of them go through a kind of grief and even anger for not having been told that there was more to the gospel than just being forgiven and waiting for heaven for perfection. This becomes even stronger when they see that the teaching they received made them blind to what the Scriptures clearly and consistently present as not only possible but as the normal and expected result of following Jesus. They wonder why this training has been lost to the church.

But for each one that comes to this awakening there are many more who are confounded and show themselves to be powerfully conditioned for low expectations of growth in this life. I empathize with them. I held their view for many years, and it took time to trust that Jesus would work with me to learn to obey him. To me, it sounded like promoting righteousness based on good works. Besides, doesn't Jesus accept me "just as I am"?

WHY WOULD ANYONE WANT TO BE GOOD?

His question floored me. A middle-aged student in my class on 2 Peter titled "How Your Life Can Become Really Good" asked the million-dollar question of formation, "Why would anyone want to do this?" "This" was taking the teaching of Peter and applying it by doing a Virtue Walk training exercise.

His honesty was refreshing, but I could feel the tension in the class as everyone knew that he was unknowingly and unintentionally challenging the whole basis for the class. And his question was great! It was an opportunity to go deep into the depths of the transformation gap, to uncover the reduced gospel and to expose the double life of devotions devoid of character formation.

He explained why he didn't think it was necessary. "Why do so," he asked, "when I am already forgiven of my sins and have peace with God for the future? Why make such a big deal about being good? If Jesus is already our Savior, why sweat this goodness thing?" I couldn't have planned a better class curriculum for that day. It raised the question of what our experience of heaven would be if we didn't desire that experience while here on earth. And it awakened desire in the students for a life with God that could start now in our everyday lives, not just in heaven. And it showed how much our expectations for life with God had been lowered—how in 2 Peter's terms, we have been blinded to God's call for a kingdom life of moral excellence, here and now.

I didn't have to answer the student's question. The class did it for me. Many of them shared how their own lives had changed. Obviously the man will need to, like I had to myself, either become tired of how he's living now or open up to a vision of a better life. I didn't get a chance to go deeper with him on the question. I have learned not to rush or push anyone's desire to be formed or follow Jesus into his life. Such a desire must come from the heart and sometimes that very question "Why do this?" is the beginning of an inner process that will take its own time, where God is slowly disturbing our temporary and earthly peace. That student has since been able to see new possibilities for his own life. But his lowered expectations due to his reduced gospel first had to be exposed.

What are our expectations for life: the lowered expectations and false comfort of the American dream, or the high and lofty reality of life in the kingdom of Jesus? And where did we get them from? Did Jesus expect that we should live without worry, anger, lust, contempt and greed? Could these sinful states cease to rule our lives? What might God accomplish in us if we became more alert and conscious of God, available to him and his power to rule in us versus being more preoccupied with ourself and meeting our own needs? And what would be the result for others if I were to become more available to them, more peaceful, and more loving and giving in our relationships.

I have not been able to shake the man's question: "Why would anyone want to do this?" Second to Kyle's question "Dad, are you home yet?" which reminds me of my own life pursuit, this one has had most of my attention lately, making me wonder how to help answer it for those who are asking.

CAN WE KNOW HOW TO OBEY?

Wondering why anyone would want to become good is a sign of how much we have lost of our biblical heritage, not only in American culture, but also in the church, even Bible-toting, born-again evangelicals. The proverb is true, for a lack of vision or knowledge the people perish (Hos 4:6). There is a loss of knowledge of how to obey that the church and our culture need to recover. The student in my class reflects a shift in our culture that puts the knowledge of good and the method for attaining it out of reach.

In *Knowing Christ Today: Why We Can Trust Spiritual Knowledge,* Dallas Willard makes the case that we no longer see morality as a legitimate field of knowledge or something one can know and experience. So our institutions of learning have no basis for helping students make moral decisions or assessments of basic good and evil. "For most of Western history, the basic claims of the Christian tradition have in fact been regarded by its proponents *as knowledge of reality*, and were presented as such." But today, educators cannot help their students become good at anything in a moral sense. I would add that most Christians, pastors and laypeople alike, have no basis for the reality of moral excellence in their lives and communities.

"It is now widely thought that there is no objective difference between a good person or a bad person, or at least that we do not know what that difference is. So, if that is true, a *method* for becoming a really good person would be presumptive and pointless." If this is true of much of the church, which I believe it is, there is no knowledge of what goodness would look like in a believer beyond the condition of being forgiven. Then a method of becoming a good person, such as the Virtue Walk, seems presumptive and pointless. But wait a second. My class was not at Harvard or the University of Illinois. It was at my church, where evangelical, Bible-believing, born-again, witnessing Christians attend. What's up with that?

The problem is that belief is no longer seen as knowledge of how to live well but is now about having the correct theological doctrine to be accepted by God into heaven.

In the church there is a gap between belief and knowledge. Beliefs that are only seen as doctrinal truths and not lived realities are "professions" of belief, a matter of lip service. These beliefs are not confessed or held close for repentant living and practice. They merely tickle the ear and mind as unused but warmly received information. Dallas goes on to apply this to the church's poverty of right living, "The difference between belief and knowledge is a difference that makes a huge difference in every area of life. Not having *knowledge* (read "experiential" here) of the central truths of Christianity is certainly one reason for the great disparity between what Christians profess and how they behave, a well known and disturbing phenomena." This defines "nominal evangelicals," those who hold their beliefs and professions in name only, not in life.

The old hymn "Trust and Obey" says it all. The only way to be happy in Jesus is to trust *and* obey. But how is that done? And who will teach us?

JESUS, WOULD YOU BE MY TEACHER?

Fred Rogers of *Mr. Rogers' Neighborhood* was a wonderful teacher. Some thieves stole a car but returned it when they found that it belonged to Mr. Rogers. They left a note with the car: "We are sorry we took your car. We didn't know it belonged to you, Mr. Rogers." Unfortunately there are not many Mr. Rogers in our society today or in the church. People whose lives are so different, whose powerful influence affects us so much that they call out the best in us.

I recall first being asked who my teacher is in life. That might seem like an unusual question since we don't live in days of rabbis or master teachers. The closest we might come to such is having a tutor in school, or a master craftsperson training us as an apprentice in some work skill, hobby or artwork. But the master-student model was the most ancient form of instruction for living a good life, and we are being reintroduced to it in the form of Muslim imams, Hindu gurus and Zen masters. Such a practice needs to be reintroduced into the church.

So who is my teacher, your teacher? One way to find out is to take a hard look at our life. Actually, most of us have had several teachers: our parents and school teachers, peers and bosses, the media and Madison Avenue advertisers, our pastors and church leaders, televangelists, and authors. When I examined my life's trail of practices and habits, I found that though I claimed Jesus as my Lord and Savior, he has not been my teacher in much of my life.

It was not until reading Dallas Willard's *Divine Conspiracy* that I discovered Jesus could be my teacher. It hit me like a ton of bricks. Jesus is the only great religious teacher who is now alive and well and giving private instruction. The classroom is not just Sunday morning at church but all of life. And the curriculum is not just a book, even the Bible, it is our lives, with all of the ups and downs, the trials and the triumphs.

Our lesson begins where we are most afraid to learn, in the places where we are broken and disobedient, where we are addicted and hooked, our habits of sin and diseased relationships with others and God. The cross and the empty tomb point to him waiting to walk and talk with us, as the old hymn "In the

Garden" says. Here we are not only forgiven of our sins but they are put to death, and we find new life. Then we follow him into the kingdom life that never ends. And soon others will be caught up in our life with Jesus.

I didn't think I could ever say what Paul said, "follow me as I follow Christ" (1 Cor 11:1 my paraphrase). I had no idea what apprenticeship to Jesus was about. My fear of works righteousness and perfectionism, and my lowered expectations of life in Christ, kept me from seeing the possibilities of being and example to others. Even my failures, when confessed and progressively overcome by cultivating new habits of obedience, can be used by Jesus as potent examples for others.

THE MARKS OF WHOLE LIFE TRANSFORMATION

The apostle Paul calls us to follow his example as he follows Christ. In 1 Corinthians 11:1 he calls out, "Follow my example, as I follow the example of Christ." If you ask most Christians if they can say this along with Paul, they would balk and say to do so they would have to be perfect. Somewhere we have lost the view of salvation as a life we can live as an example to others. Paul's letters challenge us to be living examples of Christ's life. He thought it is not only possible but the only way for salvation to be passed on.

In 1 Timothy 4:12-16 Paul calls Timothy to become an example to others of following Jesus. These verses are part of a section beginning at 1 Timothy 3:14 that is Paul's explicit instructions on how people are to conduct themselves in the church, a kind of training manual for the church. And this he makes clear by including a hymn or poem that perhaps was a part of a worship service going back to the first disciples (1 Tim 3:16). The hymn explains that the "mystery of godliness" is based on Christ's incarnation and work of redemption, which should result in the fruit of godly conduct in the church (v. 15). In chapter four Paul goes on to say that anyone who denies we can live divinely in our everyday practices of eating and drinking, and marriage and home life is listening to "deceiving spirits." Timothy, Paul says, should be an example and living illustration of godly conduct, which should have the following marks.

Qualitative difference. Timothy is to set the standard for his people by his life's example. He is to teach with his life, not just words, that godliness is possible and attainable. His leadership is not just in teaching and preaching but also apprenticing others in the best way to live. He is not expected to be perfect, but be in the process of "becoming an example" of a better life (1 Tim 4:12 my translation).

Holistic. Timothy's "speech and conduct," or words and deeds, should be formed by Christ's life (1 Tim 4:12). This theme runs throughout the New Testament, such as "Whatever you do, whether in word or deed, do it all in the name of the Lord Jesus" (Col 3:17).

Progressively better. Paul says that everyone should see Timothy's "progress." Timothy should gradually and increasingly eliminate worry and fear to such a degree that his peace will calm others. He should get rid of anger and contempt in order to love his enemies (1 Tim 4:15).

Noticeable. Timothy's progress in life is to be so evident that others cannot help but see it—like a city on a hill that cannot be hid (1 Tim 4:15). Timothy's life's is to be so powerful that it compels others to be interested in Christ. This is more caught than taught, although formal instruction is necessary too.

Worthy of imitation. "Becoming an example to the believers" (1 Tim 4:12) is a theme here and throughout Paul's writings to the church (1 Cor 4:16-17; 11:1; Phil 3:17; 1 Thess 1:6-8). Paul says Timothy should put into practice whatever has been received, learned, seen and heard in Paul. The growth of the church depends on seeing and reproducing this pattern.

More than just correct doctrine. Timothy is told, "watch your life" and doctrine too (1 Tim 4:16). But *living* the truth is referred to twice here, once before and once after urging Timothy to use Scripture. He should look at his life to see what he really believes about Scripture's teachings. He is to be diligent about his life's formation, giving himself wholly to it.

Life-situated and integrated. Timothy will continually face good and bad times, especially persecution and suffering. His godly behavior is "to persevere," to last through all circumstances and life situations. Suffering and rejection, contrary to what we may think, will form us like nothing else (1 Tim 4:16).

Lifelong. Timothy is charged to "let no one look down on his youth" and to set an example for the young and old (1 Tim 4:12). Paul didn't think anyone is too old or too young to be an example for others. Progressive and obvious growth can be ours throughout life, right up to the finish line.

Individual and corporate. Timothy is told that if he lives as Paul instructs, if he perseveres, he will be used by God and will "save both yourself and your hearers" (1 Tim 4:16), meaning he will model the reality of what only Christ made possible. The examples of Christians who obediently follow Jesus pave the way for remarkable works of saving grace, not only in Timothy's church but also whole cultures.

Let's look at someone who has done this.

MARY PRINCE: FORMER SLAVE OF CONTEMPT

Great Christians of the past not only inspire me, they are incredible teachers on how to be trained in Christlikeness. Mary Prince, a West Indies black female slave sold from a good master to a cruel and sadistic mistress, exemplifies the miraculous kind of transformation that can be achieved in this life by the practice of the disciplines.

Instead of becoming like her master, imitating her cruelty and hate, or rejecting the Christianity her masters professed but denied by their lives, Mary chose to become a follower of Jesus. Through the disciplines of prayer, confession and meditation on Scripture she learned to love her enemies and as a result was able to show respect, mercy and compassion for her torturer. Though she was abused and tortured for over thirteen years, she did not give up her dignity or pursuit of freedom, becoming a force for the abolition of slavery.

Mary describes the treatment she and others, even children, received at the hands of their "Christian" masters.

> I was kicked, and flogged, and pinched by her pitiless fingers in the neck and arms, exactly as they were. To strip me naked—to hang me up by the wrists and lay my flesh open with the cow-skin, was an ordinary punishment for even a slight offence.
>
> My mistress often robbed me too of the hours that belong to sleep. She used to sit up very late, frequently even until morning; and I had then to stand at a bench and wash during the greater part of the night, or pick wool and cotton; and often I have dropped down overcome by sleep and fatigue, till roused from a state of stupor by the whip, and forced to start up to my tasks. . . . My mistress was always abusing and fretting after me. It is not possible to tell all her ill language.

Slaveholders had a strange practice of giving their slaves ridiculous and extravagant names like Mary, Princess of Whales. This was a way to express their contempt for their slaves, but, ironically, it honored the faith and dignity of these slaves who were too holy to stoop to the contempt and foolishness of their hateful masters. While Mary prayed to live someday in liberty from her human masters, she lived in the freedom of her Lord.

Mary was converted under the influence of a Moravian church, and despite seeing the hypocrisy of those in the church, she confessed her sins and prayed for a forgiving spirit. Mary became master of her own slavery to hate and contempt, while still pursuing and finally gaining her freedom.

When Mary's story was put into print, the first story of a woman slave published in England, her former owners sued for libel. Mary sued back and won the case. Mary wrote of her attempts to be free both in status and in her spirit. In this she is a wonderful example for us.

> When I found out that I was a great sinner, I was very sorely grieved, and very much frightened. I used to pray God to pardon my sins for Christ's sake, and forgive me for every thing I had done amiss; and when I went home to my work, I always thought about what I had heard from the missionaries, and wished to be good that I might go to heaven. . . . I still live in the hope that God will find a way to give me my liberty, and give me back to my husband. I endeavour to keep down my fretting, and to leave all to Him, for he knows what is good for me better than I know myself. Yet, I must confess, I find it a hard and heavy task to do so.

She had been separated from her husband for most of her life by the will of her masters. But through it all, Mary learned to trust in God and live obediently to Christ's rule while under the harsh and crushing hand of slavery.

Mary learned to practice spiritual disciplines, which helped her to not see herself as a victim or to be consumed with rage or bitterness. She learned an obedience that freed her even while she was in a cruel, inhumane and abusive bondage. She practiced the disciplines in order to display God's power in her life and character. She became a player in the forces that brought change to the world.

In our freedom to do and act as we want in a free and richly provisioned culture, how free are we in our character? How do we use our freedom of time and will? Do we practice the disciplines to become players in God's kingdom, progressing toward our heavenly destiny of ruling in life?

PRAYER OF AUGUSTINE

Augustine trumpeted God's grace versus our works in salvation. He taught God's work for us and in us, what we cannot do for ourselves. It is ironic that evangelicals celebrate Augustine and his teaching that we will "be restless until we find our rest in God," but not his teaching on how grace transforms us and perfects us, causing us to grow in knowledge of and obedience to Jesus.

Listen to his prayer to Jesus, his Lord and Savior, and his hunger not only for resting in God's love but also for God's life and love to rest in him.

> Grant us, even us, O Lord, to know you, and love you and rejoice in you. And if we cannot do these perfectly in this life, let us, at least, advance to higher degrees every day, till we can come to do them in perfection. Let the knowledge of you increase in us here, that it may be full hereafter; that our joy may be great in itself and full in you. We know, O God, that you are a God of truth. O make good your gracious promises to us, that our joy may be full. To your honor and glory, who with the Father and the Holy Spirit lives and reigns one God, world without end. Amen.

Ruling in Kingdom Life

How could I lose my present life and gain a kingdom-sized one in which Jesus ruled? Is there a "rule of life"—a set of practices, relationships, experiences and responses to life's circumstances—that can help me to allow God to rule in my life?

I had a friend in grade school who had a strange practice he and his younger brother engaged in. Occasionally they would take all their stuff, their toys, sport equipment, games and other prized possessions and put them into two piles to see who had the most stuff. Whoever had the most stuff ruled. The winner was the family's "King of Stuff."

In the Bible whatever stuff (people, places and things) God rules over is called the kingdom of God. And in effect where he doesn't rule is a rival kingdom. Since we don't have kingdoms or kings and queens, we need examples, like my friend's strange practice, to understand what is meant by God's kingdom.

RULING YOUR OWN PILE OF DIRT

If you were to list all the stuff in your life, not just material things but your whole being—spiritual, relational, physical and emotional—and sort it into two piles, one Christ and you rule over and one ruled by sin and the world, what would be in each pile? Who would be the king of your stuff? When we talk about life in the kingdom of God, we are talking about placing *all* our stuff under the rule of God. God's kingdom is where his will is effective, where it is done. To pray "Thy kingdom come" is to ask God to reign on not only our planet but also over us, our minds, bodies and relationships. He has given us a will that, when submitted to his rule, makes of our body and life a place where his kingdom comes alive.

When I woke up from my driven life, I wasn't aware that, except for participating in church, my life was in large part under sin's rule and not God's. As I began to reexamine my life I realized that in order to live with kingdom power and effect, I needed to cooperate with God so he would rule over my life in all areas.

When we come to know Jesus and are transferred from the rival kingdom of darkness and death to his kingdom of light and life, we are given power to have God's will rule over and with our will. But this is just the beginning of a lifelong process. Though we may experience an initial and often remarkable work of God's power in an area of our life, there remains much more ground to be taken. It's God's will that our whole being—body, mind, heart and relationships—by transformed, area by area, until he rules over all.

To have this happen we need rigorous training and much practice over our lifetime. Such training requires the interruption of our current routines, the habits that got us into the kind of life we now have. The reason many Christians have such little power to rule over their bodies is that they have never undergone training. In fact, most don't know they need it. Sadly, believers are discouraged with the Christian life because no one has offered to train them to live it fully. I know, I was one.

My brother was a wrestler in high school. We all knew that when wrestling season came, his whole routine would undergo serious changes. They even effected our family routines. This didn't mean he merely practiced each day after school. But his eating and sleeping, his daily mental preparation, his schedule, in short, his everyday life was turned upside down and oriented to wrestling. His coach laid down some rules that definitely transformed his daily life. To have a hope winning a match and of making it to state competition, to that final championship match, he would have to submit to his coach's rule for his life.

QUESTIONS FOR DISCERNING A RULE OF LIFE

As I began to pursue my own transformation, I read about a kind of training for whole life transformation that reminded me of my brother's training regimen. It was called a "rule of life," a set of activities and directions that would help bring my life, my body, my pile of dirt under God's rule.

To begin to construct a rule of life I needed to look at what kind of life my practices, relationships, experiences and responses were giving me and who I was becoming. I discovered that all of us already have a rule of life, a set of activities and practices that form our present life. It's just not as intentional or conscious to us to as the rule of life I am suggesting.

After Kyle brought it to my attention, my rule was not to my liking. Those who love Christ should *really like* their life. If we don't, it is a sign that our life isn't Christ's. I gradually developed the set of questions below to help me discern the kind of life I wanted.

- Who am I *becoming?* Do I like this?

- What are the regular *practices* or habits I have given myself to?

- What *relationships* do I cultivate? Do they affect my life for good or bad?

- What kind of *experiences* and states of being am I cultivating regularly?

- What are my *responses to life's circumstances?* How are these contributing to the kind of person I am becoming?

- What *kind of life* do I have as a result of these practices, relationships, experiences and responses? Is it one others would want?

- Who is God calling me to *become?*

- What changes is God calling me to make to reach the life he wants for me?

My *practices* of prayer and Scripture weren't nourishing—I rushed through them as a duty so I could minister while medicating myself with destructive habits. I needed to slow down and learn to be with God in my practices. My *relationships* were almost entirely about church work, serving my ambition for success while neglecting my family—too busy and self-absorbed to be close to others. My *experiences* in ministry activities drained me and began to define my worth in pleasing people and performance.

And *my response to my life's circumstances* was to become so busy and driven that I lived on the surface of my life. I was numb and quietly despaired of becoming different. When Kyle woke me up from my driven pace, I found that I didn't like my life, my family didn't want it, and I was becoming someone I didn't want to be. And on top of all this, I had to face the fact that in many areas of life, I just didn't want to or intend to become what I should in Christ. I was too used to what I had become. So I needed to start where I was at, asking Jesus to first help me to want what I needed to trust him to help me become.

As I looked hard at the previous list of questions and came up with answers, I developed a basic four-part rule of life that God used to put me under his rule.

MY PERSONAL RULE OF LIFE: CORE PRACTICES
The following are the core practices of my personal rule of life:

1. Slow down to go at God's speed—the speed that honors love and relationships.

2. Pay attention to God in constant conversation, all day, every day.

3. Memorize and meditate on long passages of Scripture for life change.

4. Confess sin and receive God's forgiveness in community with a safe person or group of friends.

Through the years I have built on this basic rule with exercises like the "Virtue Walk" (pp. 139-41) and the "Corporate Rule of Life" (pp. 172-73). I had tried a smorgasbord approach to the disciplines without tying them to specific results and needed something more. So now I incorporate disciplines like solitude and silence as a part of slowing down and paying attention to God; the study of Scripture and spiritual reading as part of Scripture memory for specific life change; and examen, fellowship and celebration as part of confession of sin for loving relationships. The four core practices have a flow that leads from one to another, and as I keep cycling through, they lead to a different life. Although this list is not exhaustive, they have worked to bring slow and steady character change in me.

We can't pay attention to God, memorize his Word or confess sin without first slowing down. And when slowing down and paying attention to God isn't wed to Scripture, our slowed pace and prayer life might be fruitless. From my study, I find that the best training always involves some form of these four practices, which we will now examine in more detail.

1. *Slowing down.* As I was meditating on how to slow down my life, instead of doing a Bible study on it, I decided to do something very practical—start going the speed limit! I would no longer take that extra five to ten miles an hour the highway patrol "lets" me take. And I wouldn't use the cruise control so that the slower pace would become automatically hard-wired into my body and spirit. It worked. Going slower meant I had to back everything up in my life, from getting up earlier to leaving more time between appointments. I even started to kiss my wife goodbye again, noticing her in the morning rather than being distraught over the appointment I was late for.

The slower pace on the road put me in more of a reflective mood. I no longer had to worry about making up time for being late. I found myself becoming relaxed and less preoccupied. I use these times as openings to calm myself by being in God's presence. I learned to take whole days to just "do nothing," to rest, and I began to make more room for restorative slowing exercises. Now waiting in line at a grocery store is not an annoyance but an opportunity to be quiet and become more attuned to God. These and other slowing exercises began to bring me home to God and others. Now, when I notice I am going too fast in my car, it's time to examine what is driving me to distraction.

2. *Paying attention to God.* Going slower opened up my life to more space for God. I began to treat God like a friend who was always with me. Not just as a teacher for my morning devotions, a firefighter to put out the fires of crisis I got into or someone to acknowledge at worship services, but as my friend and teacher for every moment of life. Turning my attention to God starts in the morning and extends throughout the day at planned times for short prayers from Phyllis Tickle's *Divine Hours.* I also stop

at times to be thankful or to cast up a care, creating a kind of instant-messaging atmosphere in my heart. And I acknowledge God as my last act at night. Through this rule, I came to know the experience "what a friend we have in Jesus."

Now when I begin to isolate myself and go it alone during the day, I concretely feel God's absence. Reading Brother Lawrence, Frank Laubach and Thomas Kelly moved prayer out of my prayer closet at home and into my heart, where God always waits and often whispers or even shouts to me throughout the day. To enhance my slowing down I eliminate the noise of TV, radio, worship music and sermon CDs, and started listening to and conversing with God.

I also started practicing long periods of quiet, not trying to think about anything but allowing my mind to be still, as David says in Psalm 131, like a child with its mother. I begin to still the noise in my head and heart, the enemy's attempt to scare me to death through worry, anger or depression, or puff me up with ambition. I was able to take captive every thought and feeling, casting them to God for his keeping.

Because of my newfound awareness of Christ's presence, I discovered new power to listen to others. I still need lots of growth in this area (those who know me know I like to talk more than listen), but when I recognize Jesus as our third conversation partner, whether with just one person or a group, the conversation enters a rich kingdom frequency.

3. Memorizing and meditating on Scripture. When I first heard that a good rule for life was a commitment to memorizing longer, transformative Scripture passages, I was simultaneously intrigued and daunted. But I have memorized whole songs, so why not a long passage of Scripture. I not only recommend this to my students but require it in all my doctor of ministry classes. Most of these veteran pastors report that they feel like they are back in confirmation or Awana club. Initially they think they are too old for this kind of thing, but once they begin memorizing, it changes their lives and ministry. One pastor begrudgingly did so but found that he made his passage his preaching text, and soon his congregation was asking, "What is different about your preaching? It has come alive!" He shared his secret, and they began to do it themselves.

When we take longer passages into our body, we are doing what Paul actually did himself, letting "the word of Christ dwell in you richly as you teach and admonish one another with all wisdom, and as you sing psalms, hymns and spiritual songs" (Col 3:16). I have memorized passages like Colossians 3:1-17; 1 Corinthians 13:1-9; John 14:21-23; 2 Peter 1:1-11; and Psalms 23; 130; 131 to embody the wisdom they teach. Simply memorizing is beneficial, but when we meditate on the passage and attempt to live out it's truth, there is a formational space created that brings kingdom realities into being in our life.

I believe that Paul did the same with various psalms, like Psalm 37, which says to turn from anger that leads to lying about others and instead turn to compassion and forbearing love. This truth is reflected in Paul's letter to the Colossians. He, as it says, let the peace of God rule his stormy temper and the Word to richly dwell in him, eventually touching everything he did or said, to God's glory (Col 3:8, 16)! I find that a family or a group memorizing long passages together and then sharing what God is doing in them is one of the most powerful curriculums a church can have. When we listen to Jesus quoting Scripture we realize that this must have been one of his most basic rules of life. In fact, it has been a basic rule for the training of Christian leaders until the last one hundred years.

4. *Confession of sin and receiving forgiveness.* Confession, as I had been taught, was mainly a matter between God and me,

and no one else. And it wasn't clear to me that it also must involve confessing or agreeing as much about forgiveness as it is about our sin. When I went to my therapist and spiritual director and confessed things I had already confessed to God, and they extended grace and a word of forgiveness, I found tremendous freedom. At that point I realized the poverty of my Protestant heritage's fear of corporate confession. Unhinging confession from forgiveness and reconciliation with others has been a disservice. The safety of my therapist's and spiritual director's graciousness and love made me hungry to experience this in as many of my close relationships as possible. Spiritual direction that doesn't have a time of confession is reduced to spiritual weather reporting of my highs and lows. For true formation I need to be brutally honest with someone about my life and progress in character formation.

The gossip in our churches is a direct result of our lack of corporate confession. It counterfeits confession: we tell others about someone else's sin, rather than our own, to someone who isn't able to be part of the solution. This makes the problem bigger and allows us to ignore and stay in denial about our own sin. Thus we must be careful not to confess our sin with others unless there is an element of safety, an atmosphere of trust and grace. For years my safest place was my therapist and spiritual director. But when key relationships with others were rebuilt and ready for this practice, we mutually agreed for our need to confess our sins and graciously extend God's forgiveness.

In his classic work *Holy Living and Dying,* the seventeenth-century Anglican Jeremy Taylor presents a picture of Christian fellowship where people are lovingly and graciously straight with each other, practicing biblical exhortation and encouragement. Unlike us, they expected others to rebuke them and speak the truth in love. This was practiced so they could become better friends in Jesus, not one-upping each other spiritually. Wouldn't such a church be refreshing and inviting? Confession would not be a shameful practice to be avoided but a privileged soul-keeping exercise of love and care. I find I can easily confess sin and find forgiveness from God through someone I know has my best and eternal interest at heart.

My four-part rule of life allowed my increasing vision of life in the kingdom to become a reality in my experience. But it was soon tested and needed some beefing up in order to achieve the results I knew God was capable of bringing to me. I was faced with what some call the "graduate school of transformation"— loving my enemy.

LOVE OF A RELATIVE ENEMY

It was the last straw for me. A relative who tried to get between my wife and me had done it again—made a disparaging comment to my wife about me. So I was going to call him and finally "give him what he deserved," a piece of my mind and a good tongue lashing. He was blaming me for ruining his relationship with my wife. This was due to a confrontation my wife had with him, one suggested by her therapist, to set a boundary around talking about our marital problems. So in defending her to him, I lost it, arguing with him on the phone and even using some profanity in telling him off—which he of course reminded me wasn't too becoming for a pastor.

While writing a letter of apology to him I was dismayed at how much his hostility and my contempt and anger for him were ruling forces in my life. It had me literally by the throat and tongue. I couldn't control things I would think and then say to him. I was embarrassed by my slavery to contempt and realized how far I was from what I had been reading about the transformed life.

The animosity between us in the few times we were together

was always there, just below the surface. He would make throw-away comments that were coded attempts to keep the feud between us stoked and hot. His verbal jabs and pokes made me want to scream at him, "Just be straight with me and say it—you hate me!" The best I could do was sit there and stew or get up and leave.

And then he was diagnosed with cancer. I had made it clear to my wife that this was one family funeral I couldn't do—I would need someone to lead it so I could grieve as part of the congregation. That was my excuse, and it was a good therapeutic one, one I could hide behind.

But contempt was not just a problem with this relative, it was also an occupational hazard of being in ministry. Freedom from and power over anger and contempt was also needed at work. My work with people as a pastor and manager of staff and lay leaders often required doing some tough things, such as disciplining an employee or bearing with a lay leader who had spread their story of what had "really happened." I often justified the contempt I felt as righteous indignation. But I now understood the Bible's clear instruction to treat others as God treats us, without condemnation and contempt—even forgiving and blessing them—no matter how badly they had behaved.

So I began to apply my rule to loving my enemies. My habitual response to my enemy was felt very strongly in my body. I would run movies in my head about what I would do to get back at this relative, and I would engage him in imaginary conversations that proved my point about his behavior. But the practice of slowing down my life and being aware of God didn't let me get away with this. Saying the Lord's Prayer every morning, noon and night replaced my imaginary talks with pleas to God to "forgive me and rid me of my contempt of my relative and his contempt of me."

My memorization of Colossians 3:1-17 now had a very practical application for breaking the rule contempt had over me. Verses 8-9 that told me to "rid yourselves of all such things as these: anger, rage, malice, slander, and filthy language from your lips. Do not lie to each other." Wow! On the phone that day I experienced a downward cycle from anger that Paul describes in verses 8-9, all the way to filthy language! I had gotten *angry* with him, and instead of getting rid of the anger, I let it simmer to a *rage,* which led to *malicious* thoughts of him and *slanderous* condemnations of his entire person, finally spilling out in *filthy language.*

I asked God to rewire my responses to him when we were together so that I would turn from getting angry and practice what Paul proposed in Colossians 3:12-13: "clothe yourselves with compassion, kindness, humility, gentleness and patience. Bear with one each other and forgive whatever grievances you have against one another." So when my anger came up at something he did or said, I turned from that to *compassion* and tried to empathize with him. I returned *kind* words for his harsh words, and his negative actions with *gentleness* or *practiced patience* by offering no response. I bore his hostility and *forgave* his offenses.

Colossians goes on to explain that in taking off my old person and putting on the new, I was to see others as God now saw me. I could no longer consider people apart from who they are in Christ, made in God's image and saved by Christ's death. I couldn't write my relative off. In fact, according to the kingdom charter, the Sermon on the Mount, I was to do the opposite, blessing him when he mistreated me and interceding for his blessing as well. So during my regular prayer time I viewed him as made in God's image and recalled his good qualities rather than those that irritated me. I imagined him as he could be in Christ, and prayed that by God's grace he would become the best he could be.

I began to pray for my enemies, with him at the top of the list, and imagined them blessed and better. For some time now I have blessed both friends and enemies equally. This is the direct result of learning to love my hated relative, and is just one practice in a set aimed at conquering my contempt and hatred of others. In wonderful answer to my prayers, I have seen enemies become friends. My relative is one.

Once when praying for him I felt moved to visit him, if he would let me. He was suspicious at first, wondering why I was interested in him, but after lots of small talk and then his opening up to me about his illness, we were able to pray together. I asked his forgiveness for the contempt I had for him, not waiting for or getting anything back, and proceeded to ask God's blessing on him. As I blessed him, the contempt was slowly being killed off even though he had given no sign of being sorry for anything he had done.

Then the real test came. He asked me to do his funeral and look after his family. I felt the leftover contempt in me starting to rise, and I started to silently protest to God about doing his funeral. My relative then said, "Let's just say everything between us is water over the bridge." In other words, ignore it! It was then that my practice paid off. I found that I had power over the rising contempt, and I chose to love, forgive and bless him.

With gratitude for God's grace, I heard myself saying yes to both requests, to go beyond being locked up in the past or my need for his apology, and to bless him by doing his funeral and caring for his family. It wasn't forced or white-knuckled. It was just what I had asked Jesus to help me do. Ministering to his family at the funeral was a joy, and caring for them now is a blessing.

THE RULE OF AMERICAN IDOLATRY

I enjoy watching *American Idol* with my family. We pick who we think is going to win and love to see the winner's wild ride to fame and fortune. Simon Cowell's trashing of self-absorbed wannabe contestants, his putdowns of Paula Abdul, who gives each performance a standing ovation, and Randy Jackson's "dog" talk makes for a great evening of brainless entertainment. After one particularly cruel evaluation of a tearful and humiliated singer, I got all serious, much to the chagrin of my kids, and interrupted the show by asking them what *American Idol* was forming in our own souls and in our culture.

They didn't have a clue, and neither did I. And after the usual, "It's just a show, Dad," we resumed watching. Perhaps the show is just a time of vegging before the TV. But the next day's newspaper happened to have an editorial commenting on the effect of reality shows on the average viewer.

The columnist wondered if we were being exposed to and taken in by "leering cruelty." He postulated that reality-show viewers are voyeurs who are unconsciously learning to become more and more critical of others, especially those who don't conform to the idolized perceptions of culture. Might this be a reason why we have zero tolerance policies at schools and lessons on tolerance in a culture where civility is being all but removed? Television viewing takes up more of our time than most of us would like to admit. And most of our commercials rely on lust, greed and immediate gratification to motivate us to buy products with built-in obsolescence. Aren't television, movies and the Internet (or the regular use of any media) spiritual practices that form us? In the last quarter of 2008 the average American watched TV for 151 hours a month, which was up five hours from the same period in 2007. That is five hours a day! We may not be paying attention the whole time the TV is on, but it literally forms us as we practice its presence.

I have a friend who when seeing someone reading the daily

newspaper asks, "So, what is new with the world, the flesh and the devil?" Even though you might not think you have a rule of life already in place, you do. You might not call it that, but something, some rule, leads you to live in God's trinitarian kind of life or the alternative trinity of the world, the flesh and the devil.

A couple of the young men I mentor (and a friend of theirs) have recently turned off their TVs for good (except for the Vikings football). Instead of watching TV shows, they are reading a book about practicing God's presence and attempting to live it out, discussing the results one night a week. Their new practice has resulted in greater obedience to God. Subsequently, they have become more attentive to others and less consumed with the need to be entertained.

I have my seminary students do the previous exercises to have them find out what is ruling their life and how they might change it. I ask them to list the relationships they cultivate, practices or habits they engage in, experiences they give themselves to and their responses to life circumstances. Addictions and compulsive habits like TV, pornography, shopping, Internet surfing or texting qualify as practices as much as Bible study or prayer. Experiences such as fits of rage and anger or worry and fear qualify as much as centering prayer and meditation. Then they are to identify who their teachers are and what their vision for life is.

One student admitted that American culture and evangelicalism had taught him to pursue success, which is measured by growing a large church. He said he took my course on spiritual formation in order to make himself more successful. He also admitted that he went to the Bible for sermons and not for feeding his soul, that his marriage was suffering from his preoccupation with ministry, and his prayer life was nonexistent. (Many more students confided that they coped with stress by addictive

behavior and habitual sins that they were ashamed of. They
longed to be free.)

This particular student chose to replace his current rule with
another one that has Jesus as Teacher and kingdom life as its vision. He and his wife pursued counseling and experienced new
life together. His prayer life became rich and full, and his sermons came alive with the Scripture's transformational message
of life in the kingdom. His congregation commented on the new
power in his preaching and teaching. When they observed that
he had memorized and meditated his way into this new power,
many imitated his practice for change in their own lives.

CORPORATE RULES OF LIFE

Though I kept my own rule of life between me and my director,
some of the church staff noticed the changes in my life. They
asked if they could experience some of the things I had at the
retreat center I attended. At first I was reluctant to do this, fear-
ing that this sacred space where God had met me would be
taken over by the work of ministry, and I would lose what I had.
But as we talked we decided to try a retreat for the staff to experience quiet and the rhythms of slowing down.

So I developed and led an annual "Wasting Time with God
and Others" retreat. It is wasting time with God because no
work or cell phones are allowed. We do nothing much but be
with God and each other (which is really something quite extraordinary!). The entire staff, not just the pastoral staff, enjoy
slowing things down and being together for a couple of days.
We made a habit of going to same retreat center at the same time
each year in order to develop a rhythm for the new year by getting away to be with God.

I started each retreat with what has become my mantra: "The
greatest enemy of intimacy with God is service for God." We

practiced a form of prayer that involves stilling the mind, heart and body, which was a welcome "intervention" on ourselves since we are in such a hurry to do things *for* God, not *with* him. Though the retreat was taken at the busiest time of the year, just before the fall kickoff, the days weren't filled with planning presentations, teachings, team exercises or professional training. Twice a day, we read a small passage of Scripture and then sat quietly for twenty minutes. To others the retreat might have looked like a total waste of time for busy church leaders. But we knew better.

Being quiet for a few days sets a base line of dependency on God for the whole year. We need to create "sacred space and time" in our everyday lives and establish sacred rhythms of regular disengagement from ministry to reengage our life with God. This rhythm was reinforced in staff meetings throughout the year when we came together for quiet and reflection.

I found that the staff began to incorporate practices learned at retreat into their everyday lives. An administrative assistant incorporated the practice of quiet in her morning drive to work, turning off the radio and being silent for the whole drive. Pastors began sitting in quiet during their preparation time for sermons. Other staff used Phyllis Tickle's *Divine Hours* regularly.

We also brought some of the practices into church board meetings. Time was set aside in the agenda so that the high-energy give and take of business was grounded in God's agenda and not just ours.

Starting the day by being quiet for five to twenty minutes and adding divine hours or short appointments to turn to God throughout our day is quantitatively and qualitatively different than the quick shots of prayer in the typical quiet time or opening prayers of business meetings. We typically ask God to bless our day or meeting, but we don't stop long enough or be still enough to hear God's voice above our own.

The retreat is an example of a rule of life that can be applied to a whole group, but it also can be applied to other areas of community life. At Open Door we began to experiment with a corporate rule of life for our various teams. The vision was that it would eventually be used in the training and ongoing ministry practice of all our leaders, becoming a way of life for the community that is more caught than taught.

A CORPORATE RULE OF LIFE (FOR STAFF AND LAY LEADERS)

The following rule of life is an example of the kind of an expanded corporate rule. I have used this in my contexts as well as with a number of other pastors and churches in their staff and lay teams. This rule covers more than just the traditional spiritual practices of prayer and Scripture use. It also addresses the need to "speak the truth in love" (Eph 4:15) so that our interactions are more about building the body of Christ into maturity rather than tearing the body apart by our usually petty criticisms. We will not tolerate gossip, slander or innuendo. Instead, the rule leads us to think the best of others and consider them better than ourselves (Phil 2:3-4).

We are to submit ourselves to others and the group's direction even when we do not agree with it. In this, we are not giving up our first obedience to God, but believe God speaks to us through his beloved community. Their loving wisdom or even correction and rebuke provide a kind of low-level discipline that precludes most grievous and drastic forms of sin. This rule has nipped affairs in the bud by noticing poor boundaries that can lead to improper relationships. It holds others accountable before serious damage is done to families and spouses.

The following is an example of a corporate rule.

1. Living in Jesus. We will develop habits of "being with Jesus" for transformation into trinitarian life. We will incorporate such practices as

- slowing our lives down together to eliminate hurry
- together paying attention to God all day, every day
- memorizing and meditating together on transformative passages of Scripture
- confessing our sins to one another in safe groups or with directors

2. Living in transformation. We will intentionally and freely speak the truth to each other for everyone's good in all areas of our lives as individuals and groups, and in our organization.

3. Living in community. We will remain with each other and do life together, not submitting to institutional isolation and the slow death of going too fast or being too busy to love each other.

4. Living in mission. We will be in the world, but not of it. We will serve (and be served by) those around us, but particularly the least and last and the overlooked. We will consider others better than ourselves.

5. Living in reconciliation. Though we expect conflict and disorder in our relationships, we refuse to live in unresolved conflict and will practice the peace of Christ among us.

6. Living in good speech. We will always believe and speak the best about each other and not entertain rumors, gossip, demeaning talk or slander. We will bring bad reports about a person directly to him or her for answer and response.

7. Living in submission to one another. We will submit to one another in love, believing that by God's grace our community has the wisdom we need to live by. But we will not allow submission to each other to take the place of submitting to God.

Such corporate rules of life have been the secret for the formation of powerful communities of transformation throughout history. In *Alternative to Futility*, D. Elton Trueblood notes:

> [Jesus] did not form an army, establish headquarters, or write a book. What he did was to collect a few very common men and women, inspire them with the sense of his spirit and vision, and build their lives into an intensive fellowship of affection, worship, and work.
>
> One of the truly shocking passages of the gospel is that in which Jesus indicates that there is absolutely no substitute for the tiny, loving, caring, reconciling society. If this fails, he suggests, all is failure; there is no other way. He told the little bedraggled fellowship that they were actually the salt of the earth and that if this salt should fail there would be no adequate preservative at all. He was staking all on one throw.
>
> What we need is not intellectual theorizing or even preaching, but a demonstration. One of the most powerful ways of turning people's loyalties to Christ is by loving others with the great love of God. We cannot revive faith by argument, but we might catch the imagination of puzzled men and women by an exhibition of a fellowship so intensely alive that every thoughtful person would be forced to respect it. If there should emerge in our day such a fellowship, wholly without artificiality and free from the dead hand of the past, it would be an exciting event of momentous importance. A society of genuine loving friends, set free from the self-seeking struggle for personal prestige and from all unreality, would be something utterly priceless and powerful. A wise person would travel any distance to join it.

Dietrich Bonhoeffer's *Life Together* and Thomas à Kempis's *Imitation of Christ* say much the same. These men were formed by community rules of life powerful enough to counteract the drag of our broken world. And others were caught up in the their transformed lives.

Committed groups arise wherever Jesus' teaching and life is taken seriously. Whether it is Francis of Assisi's band of wandering brothers, John and Charles Wesley's holy club, or Walter Rauschenbusch's Brotherhood of the Kingdom, Jesus' presence creates small groups of committed followers who want to experience kingdom community.

Families, small groups, ministry teams and church boards have this potential. But they have to break through the isolation of living "alone together." Author Thomas Kelly draws a line between those who want only half of what Jesus brings and those who want complete kingdom life. Some of us want to feel religious but don't want to follow Jesus in complete obedience. But when a group of like-minded and devoted followers of Jesus get together and carry each other in wordless prayer, they become "weighty friends" whose influence on each other fires the hot pursuit of God. They constitute what Kelly calls "the Fellowship," which is mostly invisible to the world and even the church. He believes that the webs of these various groups also carry God's kingdom plan for humanity, embodying and inviting others to enter in.

God's plan for kingdom rule is for groups of followers of Jesus—couples, families, friends and informal groups scattered throughout homes, churches, businesses, schools and other institutions—to repeat the pattern that Jesus modeled to the first disciples. Often these groups coalesce around a single flame, a torch of a well-lived life, that ignites others to follow Jesus' pattern of conduct.

The concept of having a rule of life is not familiar to most evangelical Christians. For some the word *rule* may imply legalism or moralism. And we all know of churches, institutions or groups with lists of prescribed or banned behaviors that did not bring life but the opposite, allowing sin to enslave further. A rule of life is no good in and of itself, but only if it helps us move into kingdom life. A good rule of life helps us "rule in life," and the best ones become embodied in the group's common experience as Christ's body.

A corporate rule can be used informally, in everyday interactions between employees, and also more formally, in orienting new staff and evaluating performance. My report forms have a section to report on progress on work goals, but also one on how specific rules are being lived out. In the context of the rule on submitting, one staff member reported that he had chosen not to push back when our tech people didn't fulfill his request to have his computer changed from a PC to a Mac. He could have made an issue of it but felt God's leading to accept their decision.

PRACTICING TOGETHER TO PLAY TOGETHER

Corporate rules of life are what author Scot McKnight calls for, communal practices, not just solo disciplines. He notes that although his high school basketball coach had each team member doing free throws on his own at home, the athletes spent most of their time on the court practicing together. Somehow we in the church have isolated our formation to what we do as individuals, and then we wonder why our communities have no or little formational power for transforming relationships. There is a contradiction in attempting to impart and sustain trinitarian life mainly through isolated and individualized practice.

A practice of the college I went to was a powerful influence on me. We often sang the school hymn, "May the Mind of Christ My Savior," in chapel and at special occasions like commencement and graduation. I fondly remember singing it and the message it embodies. Kate B. Wilkinson wrote its five verses as a rule of life for her students, reminding them of Christ's mindset.

The hymn's words incorporate Colossians 3:1-17, Ephesians 3:14-21 and 2 Timothy 4:1-8, transformational passages worth memorizing and meditating on as a rule of life.

Each school day Kate's students memorized a verse of the hymn, using it for meditation and practice:

Monday
May the mind of Christ, my Savior,
Live in me from day to day,
By His love and power controlling, all I do and say.

Tuesday
May the Word of God dwell richly
In my heart from hour to hour
So that all may see I triumph
Only through His power.

Wednesday
May the peace of God my Father
Rule my life in everything
That I may be calm to comfort
Sick and sorrowing.

Thursday
May the love of Jesus fill me
As the waters fill the sea,
Him exalting, self abasing,
This is victory.

Friday
May I run the race before me
Strong and brave to face the foe,
Looking only unto Jesus
As I onward go.

9

Leaving the
Results to God

How *do I now measure ministry success if not in just attendance,
buildings and budgets? What is success, and how did Jesus and Paul
view success as they approached the "finish line," their last days on
earth? How should we live each day with that finish line in mind?*

I had prayed through my day that morning. That is, I looked at
all my appointments I had for the day and presented them to
God. I try to begin each day with God, not just during my quiet
time but in a moment by moment, day-long partnership with
him. And before each event of the day, I place that event, person, decision, project or activity in God's presence and hands. I
have learned to be open to interruptions by God through unplanned appointments or his nudging me to do something not
on my schedule.

I had a big talk to give that evening at our church's annual
business meeting. We were introducing a new approach in outreach and evangelism. I had some ideas of what to say but had
no time until that day to put it on paper. I usually keep my office
door open, but I shut myself in for the day. After some morning
meetings, I was ready to write. We were going to live in a manner that raised questions, practicing God's presence and follow-

ing his lead. But this approach needed to be explained thoughtfully, and I had to put forth my best effort in presenting it.

Just as I was making progress, there was a knock on my door. Hiding my annoyance with a smile, I said, "Come on in." The door cracked open to reveal a face I had never seen before. The man sheepishly asked, "Do you know where pastor so-and-so's office is? I have an appointment for prayer with him and can't find it." Relieved, I gave him directions and got back to writing about evangelism at the church.

OPEN TO GOD'S INTERRUPTIONS

A few minutes later brought another knock on the door. And now the stranger asked, "Would you pray with me? Pastor so-and-so isn't in."

Just as I was about to say no or redirect him to another pastor, I felt a strong leading that I should pray with this person. After a split-second's deliberation, I heard myself saying, "Come in and sit down. I would be glad to pray with you." My practice of praying to notice when God was interrupting had just invaded my agenda.

The stranger, Damon, served a spiritual fastball question that is so easy to hit. "I am so lost. My life is empty. There is something about the people here, the messages, the singing. I am not used to any of it, being used to church being boring, but I just come and cry the whole time. What is going on? Can you help me get close to God? I have done some things that are really bad—treated my girlfriend rotten—and want to live differently. Can you help me?" After some more conversation, and explaining what it means to follow Jesus, he prayed to ask Jesus to be his teacher in life and to forgive him, be his Lord, Savior and friend. The whole thing took a half hour.

Now I don't live like this all the time. I am not as conscious of God as I'd like. But I have experienced this way of living often enough that I know now that if I simply obey God and leave my day in his hands, wonderful things, supernatural things, take place. If I lived as if it were all up to me, I wouldn't accomplish or see half of what I do. So I lost about thirty minutes of prep time I had set aside. When I returned to writing, the talk—outline, title and all—came in about fifteen minutes! I marveled at how great it is to work with God and leave the results to him.

My evangelism presentation that night was no problem. In fact, it was inspired. God had a different idea of how to prepare me, showing me what was most important in my day and how to trust him when he leads in ways I don't expect. But this doesn't mean I expect God to magically help me with all my preparations. I prepare as much as or more than ever. But I have learned that the best preparation for each day is to practice his presence, following his lead and leaving the results to him.

IT'S UP TO GOD, NOT ME

Two of my favorite phrases from Dallas Willard are "leave the results to God" and "don't sweat it" in life or ministry. Taking that instruction seriously has meant that I don't worry about what happens. I just make sure I am living in Jesus and doing things with him. Being with him and following where he leads is the success I seek. Jesus called his disciples to his easy yoke. Life and ministry in cooperation with Jesus has a rhythm that allows the soul to rest. Jesus says, "Watch how I do it. Learn the unforced rhythms of grace. I won't lay anything heavy or ill-fitting on you. Keep company with me and you will learn to live freely and lightly" (Mt 11:29-30 *The Message*).

When I am stressed as a way of life, not just the occasional time when things get busy, I almost always start to lose my habit of praying through my day. I go it alone. Jesus doesn't give us more to do. He doesn't make us perform. I put heavy and ill-fitting things on myself. There is more than enough time to do the things God calls me to do. Some of our organizations are stressed because their leaders are not cooperating with God. They are living as if the results were up to them. But when we leave the results to God, we get more done. We need to learn to accept Jesus' easy yoke.

Jesus' easy yoke is illustrated by the way a horse is trained to plow. An older, more experienced horse is teamed with a young and inexperienced horse. The young horse will try to go faster than the older horse, pushing against the yoke, attempting to do too much by itself. And this continues until the frenetic horse tires out and learns the gentle and easy rhythm of the trained horse. It learns to share the load. Jesus similarly wants to share our load and teach us how to work with him.

The yoke of my son, family, friends, therapist, spiritual director and coworkers stopped me. I certainly am not fully trained yet, but I have slowed down enough to allow Jesus to pull more of my weight. I try not to get ahead of or lag behind him as much as I had.

This way of living leaves room for others to be influenced by God's Spirit as I simply play my own part, not worrying about God's part or that of others. Space is allowed for God to work, and there is tremendous freedom in this. Before, I was doing things myself and was getting in the way of God and of others, including myself. God respects our wills, gently waiting for us to get tired of doing things by ourselves and are ready for a different way.

As I gave up control of my life and trusted God for the outcomes, I discovered a newfound freedom to be present to God and others in love. When we have to come up with answers for everyone we meet, we do not listen to them. We are always figuring out what to do for them instead of listening to them and to God. This even affected my sermon preparation. I no longer worried about losing a significant thought I had for a sermon. I could read Scripture or a book knowing that God would bring to me what he wanted. I simply prayed the new thought back at God for his keeping. Using prayer as a notebook always brought back those ideas that had weight and refined them in a way that my solo ruminations didn't.

I began to spend much more time praying for those I speak to, teach or work with rather than worrying about my talk or writing. I believe praying my material and interceding for those I am addressing is similar to Paul's reminders to his readers that he remembered them often in prayer. Doing this puts our material in God's hands, and it thereby has more power and more effect.

At the time that I began a practice of starting my day with Jesus, I would often use a picture of Jesus that my spiritual director suggested as I prayed. I needed a new image because, as a child I was frightened more than comforted by a large picture of Jesus that hung behind the pulpit of our church. It was a popular painting called *Head of Christ* by Warner Sallman. Jesus stares off into space, distant and unavailable, unsmiling and unearthly. To me this painting represents not only the Christ of the reduced gospel but also the absence of Jesus in daily life. The new picture that my spiritual director suggested I use isn't culturally correct. I call it "GQ Jesus" due to the Brad Pitt face, vanilla but tan, and hair. But this Jesus whose smiling face welcomes me is inviting me to live every day in his presence and power. The bright and easygoing eyes look deep into mine as if to say, "What are we going to do today? Who are we going to bless? What good can we do together?"

WHEN YOU JUST KNOW, YOU KNOW

When they partnered with God, Paul and others developed a confidence that allowed them to patiently wait for the kind of results they came to expect from God. They first experienced this in their own lives, seeing God supernaturally change their own anger, worry and lust. Then they saw God work through them to help others be transformed. Paul confidently called others to live free of sin because he knew the power of God in his own life. So much of our preaching is weak because we are doing it by our own power of persuasion rather than testifying to what we know from personal experience, as the Bible says, "Taste and see that the LORD is good" (Ps 34:8).

Paul was power crazy as a result. Not with the kind of power lust we see in those who try to control and manipulate others. Paul's desire was to know the fullest measure of Christ—the power of his resurrection and the fellowship of his sufferings. His prayer that the Ephesians would experience Christ's power and love more than they could ask or imagine (Eph 3:20) was based on his own experience. He prays that we too will share his own experience of Christ dwelling in him. As a result, he received the character that God could trust with resurrection power and results.

When we have experienced God's resurrection power and have a clear taste of heaven in this life, we receive freedom and confidence that are other-worldly. It is the stuff that makes for martyrs, both "red" (who suffer and give their lives) and "white" (who seek God's kingdom as aliens and strangers in the world). Either way, we see our own work for God on earth slip away like a morning dew burned away by the scorching winds of this world's fiery testing—but know that none of it is lost.

Maximillian Kolbe, a priest and martyr during WWII, had this confidence. He had no fear of death and was used by God to help others face theirs. He ended up in a Nazi concentration camp in the final days of WWII. One day, as the Allied troops were just miles away from liberating the camp, Kolbe offered to take the place of a young father who was to be punished with a slow and horrific death. With the Allies approaching, he and others were executed. But they were already free, having left their lives in God's hands.

THIS LIFE: SPRING TRAINING FOR ETERNITY

Through their lives, Paul and Maximillian Kolbe teach us that this life is not the sum total of our existence. In fact, this life is only a brief beginning stage of eternity. It's like Major League Baseball's spring training, which is only preparation for the season of real play. Preseason games don't count the same as the regular season, but they do serve a purpose: they test to see who will qualify for various positions on the team. And life on earth tests us to see who will be trusted with different kinds of responsibility.

My confidence was tested as I followed Jesus. Trusting him for results meant staying in training even though I seemed to become worse. As I found how unformed I was, the fight for my formation was in full force. Outward behaviors can be churned out fairly quickly, but the heart and inner character are formed over time with a lot of trial and error.

Paul was very patient with his churches, which at the end of his life didn't look very successful. He trusted that God's work in them was being carried out supernaturally; whatever he planted in the soil of God's kingdom would not fail to produce. Paul's confidence in the spread of the gospel in spite of tremendous setbacks is quite amazing. His vision of where God was taking the gospel showed how thoroughly Paul had tasted God's goodness and power. He *knew* that in spite of what he was able to see, God's purposes would prevail.

Dietrich Bonhoeffer, whose costly discipleship was marked by specific obediences, reminds us that "like the Christian's sanctification, Christian community is a gift of God to which we have no claim. Only God knows the real condition of either our community or our sanctification. What may appear weak and insignificant to us may be great and glorious to God."

So we leave the results to God. This has changed my view of success. I no longer worry about attendance numbers and the typical measures of ministry success in buildings, budgets, how well known I am or how well known are the people I hang with. Success is faithfully following Jesus wherever he calls me. A respected Christian leader told me that he knew few Christian leaders who finished well. Yes, he referred to many that had fallen but more that were just tired, bitter or disappointed. When we leave the results to God and enjoy him as our reward—no matter what happens—we will never be disappointed or need to fall for sin's reward.

What is the measure of success when we slow down and start practicing the rhythms of grace—knowing God's life so well that nothing else can shake our confidence? What can we expect when we don't measure success by numbers and activity, which wax and wane?

There are two examples in Scripture that I look to when I think of finishing well, even when the visible results aren't in sight. They lived in the vision of God—the reality of experiencing life in the kingdom of God. They knew in their bones what is true, which gave them great confidence.

Two Views from Life's Finish Line

Looking back on his life with Christ, Paul says,

The time has come for my departure. I have fought the

good fight, I have finished the race, I have kept the faith. Now there is in store for me the crown of righteousness, which the Lord, the righteous Judge, will award me on that day—and not only to me, but also to all who have longed for his appearing. (2 Tim 4:6-8)

He was not expecting to get into heaven and begin to be transformed there. Paul uses the images of a race and a fight to describe his journey with Christ, a life spent in training for godliness. Keeping the faith is more than believing the right doctrines and defending the truth of the gospel, it is living for Christ and obeying him in this life.

Paul faces God, his righteous Judge, with Christ's righteousness, not just as his ticket into heaven but as the curriculum of his own life's training (2 Tim 3:16). He expects a "crown of righteousness" or the full experience of godliness, which he has longed for and lived for his whole life.

At the end, Paul looked like a failure and was deserted by many of his own followers. Much of his life was full of pain and rejection. But suffering, he tells us, is not only to be endured but to be expected by those who live a godly life in Christ. Though he has suffered, he is content because he has gained in godliness and has been trained in righteousness. Even though he has only food and clothing, he is richer than anyone.

Paul's idea of a successful Christian life is very different from ours. No large following or organizational success validated him. No acclaim or fame was his before he died. And yet he was so sure of his life's meaning and effectiveness, due to the gospel's power, that he faced death glorifying God for every day he served on earth.

His last words bring to mind the last words of Jesus: "It is finished" (Jn 19:30). Jesus too viewed life from his finish line and saw that the religious world would call the way he lived and died a failure. These words—"It is finished"—have been interpreted theologically and linguistically as referring mostly to his payment for sins, so he is saying that our sin penalty is "paid in full." The root word means something much more than this, however. It refers to his life work, not just the few hours on the cross. He embodied the Torah as the Word of God; through his life everyone is given life. He finished or fulfilled the mission God gave to him. In addition to dying for our sins, he showed us how to live and die. Jesus too had run the race, fought the good fight and kept the faith.

About the sinless One, the writer of Hebrews says,

> During the days of Jesus' life on earth, he offered up prayers and petitions with loud cries and tears to the one who could save him from death, and he was heard because of his reverent submission. Although he was a son, he learned obedience from what he suffered and once made perfect, he became the source of eternal salvation for all who obey him. (Heb 5:7-9)

He came to earth not only to die for our sins and take death away, but to show us and teach us how to live.

EMPTY-HANDED FAITH, UNATTACHED LOVE, HOPELESS HOPE

One of my favorite songwriters is Bruce Cockburn. He writes about the spiritual life like no other I know. His songs evidence a faith that isn't conditioned by sight but by a vision from eternity. His faith is not satisfied with pie in the sky, but spurs him on to call others to help usher in the kingdom, which he believes will come. Being with the world's poor and oppressed in countries devastated by the West's machinations hasn't jaded him but pushes him deeper into the possibilities he can see by faith—"kicking against the darkness" in sure hope of the coming light.

In *Dark Night of the Soul,* Gerald May presents the triad of faith, love and hope in a way that shows he knows how to live by leaving the results to God. He invites us to live long and hard into God's reality, letting go of our own ways and exercising an "empty-handed" faith and becoming useful to God. He talks of an "unattached love" that is progressively detached from everything but God and is then free to love all things and everyone. Finally, he describes a "hopeless hope," which in the midst of no evidence of any hope, still hopes, and then hopes again and again.

WHEN THE KINGDOM BREAKS OUT IN SUCCESS

Probably the toughest time to trust God with our results is when we are successful. We are tempted to think that we are the source of what is happening. We take the serpent's advice that put an end to Adam and Eve's easy yoke with God, to think we have arrived and can go it alone now. So many ministries have peaked with God's help and then sputtered by forgetting to continue to rely on God. The good kings of Israel weren't brought down by their failures; these caused them to trust God more. But then something set in that tempted them to "take a vacation from God," which soon became a lifestyle.

Let's look at historical examples of those who stayed faithful in the success of kingdom work.

In the mid-nineteenth century Johann and Christoph Blumhardt, a father and son duo, pastored in Germany and later came to influence theologians like Karl Barth and Dietrich Bonhoeffer with their vision of God's kingdom. The elder Blumhardt had an uneventful ministry until he came upon a demon-possessed young lady in his congregation. Paranormal manifestations were also evident in the house and then in a sister. He prayed for over two years but saw nothing change—things got worse! His resolve undaunted, he exclaimed to God, "We have seen what the devil can do, now let us see what Jesus can do." He continued to pray, claiming her body, mind, heart and soul as well as her house and sister for Christ. Finally, when things were the worst, the sister, in a voice not her own, shrieked, "Jesus is victor!" and the demons were gone.

The Blumhardts believed that a demon had cried out this admission of defeat as it left the girl. Jesus as Victor became their theme and led them to a renewed study of Scripture. They developed a view of God's kingdom as being present and available now. The Blumhardts started a fellowship in Bad Boll, Germany, which came to influence the next generation contributing to the formation of the Bruderhof, a community still in existence today. (Curiously, Walter Rauschenbusch and his friends called themselves the Brotherhood of the Kingdom at about the same time.) Their lives influenced many, although America would not feel their influence because Germany's influence here waned due to the World Wars. But it would be felt by Bonhoeffer and others, who called the church to count the cost of being Jesus' disciples now, not just in heaven.

The elder Blumhardt's new kingdom theology is best found in his own words.

> There must be a new reality which is of the truth. It is not to be a new doctrine or law, not a new arrangement. The new truth to which we must listen is that which came in the person of the Son of Man himself, namely, that God is now creating a new reality on earth, a reality to come first among men but finally over all creation, so that the earth and the heavens are renewed. God is creating something new. A new history is starting. A new world is coming to earth.

Christoph Blumhardt gave up his successful healing ministry after finding that character formation was being overshadowed by miracles. The healings quietly continued but Christoph believed "it was more important to be cleansed than healed . . . to have a heart for God's cause . . . not to be chained to the world but be able to move for the Kingdom of God." He went on to engage in politics, serving a term as a legislator. He eventually grew disillusioned with political power games, but not his political ideals. His motto became "Wait and Hasten." His understanding of "hasten" was that the call of the Christian is still for him to give himself completely to the cause of the kingdom, to do everything in his power to help the world toward that goal. Yet, at the same time, a Christian must remain calm and patient, unperturbed even if his efforts show no sign of success, willing to "wait" for the Lord to bring the kingdom at his own pace and in his own way.

KINGDOM TIMING: WAIT AND HASTEN!

The Blumhardt's "wait and hasten" posture is expanded on by Latin American priest Oscar Romero, who gave himself fully to the "already but not yet" of the kingdom's advance and participation in it. He steps back to remind himself that this kingdom is not one he or we can bring in our own efforts. This is remarkable in that he was seen by some as advocating a particular kind of liberation theology. He speaks to us in a form of prayerful meditation:

It helps, now and then, to step back and take a long view.

The kingdom is not only beyond our efforts, it is even beyond our vision.

We accomplish in our lifetime only a tiny fraction of the magnificent enterprise that is God's work. Nothing we do is complete, which is a way of saying that the

kingdom always lies beyond us.
No statement says all that could be said.
No prayer fully expresses our faith.
No confession brings perfection.
No pastoral visit brings wholeness.
No program accomplishes the church's mission.
No set of goals and objectives includes everything.

This is what we are about. We plant the seeds that one
day will grow.
We water seeds already planted,
knowing that they hold future promise.

We lay foundations that will need further development.
We provide yeast that produces far beyond our capa-
bilities.

We cannot do everything, and there is a sense of liberation in realizing that.
This enables us to do something, and to do it very well. It
may be incomplete, but it is a beginning, a step along
the way, an opportunity for the Lord's grace to enter
and do the rest.

We may never see the end results, but that is the difference between the master builder and the worker.

We are workers, not master builders; ministers, not
messiahs. We are prophets of a future not our own.
Amen.

Martin Luther King Jr. is another martyr who lived in the
"wait and hasten" mode. He *waited* by turning from violence,
and *hastened* by preaching, boycotting and striking. Many of
my African American friends told me that the day Barack Obama,

the first president of color, was elected, they saw King's example as the force that turned a racist country into one in which a white majority would elect a black person to the most powerful office in the world.

Can we learn to plant everything we do in the unseen ground of God's kingdom, his field of dreams, that will bring forth fruit just as surely as Jesus rose from the grave and the new heavens and earth will come. Let us do God's will in spite of what we see and how we are treated. Let us do it anyway.

Mother Teresa's words similarly remind us to confidently believe that God will complete what we do, in spite of what others do, even their resistance to or undoing of what we have placed in God's kingdom soil.

People are often unreasonable, irrational and self-centered. Forgive them anyway.

If you are kind, people may accuse you of selfish ulterior motives. Be kind anyway.

If you are successful, you will win some unfaithful friends and some genuine enemies. Succeed anyway.

If you are honest and sincere, people may deceive you. Be honest and sincere anyway.

What you spend years creating, others could destroy overnight. Create anyway.

If you find serenity and happiness, some may be jealous. Be happy anyway.

The good you do today will often be forgotten. Do good anyway.

Give the best you have, and it will never be enough. Give your best anyway.

In the final analysis, it is between you and God. It was never between you and them anyway.

PAYDAYS IN MINISTRY, TURNS IN LIFE

Although the Scriptures speak of "rewards," or what I term "paydays in life," evangelicals, perhaps afraid of works salvation, rarely refer to this formational image often used by Jesus and Paul. Nothing I do in cooperating with God in my sanctification or formation is something I have earned or received on my own. All of it is a gift of grace from God. But we do have a part in our formation, and in this life we have formational paydays. I have received rewards in the lives of my family and church.

Paydays come for those in God's service. When our kids grow up and we are empty nesters, we have either enjoyable relationships with our spouse and grown children or a ministry that has robbed us of that. When we retire, we find out if we have friends or just former work associates. We discover if we have life *with* God or we were just doing things *for* him. Hopefully we will have a rich and full union of wills and hearts, the fruit of doing things with God, not just for him.

Paul Tournier refers to the payday of retirement and finding out what we really have:

> The die is cast. That which I have been able to learn, or to acquire is gradually losing its value. The *doing* and *having* are giving way to the *being*. What is important for the aged is not what they are still able to do, nor yet what they have accumulated and cannot take with them. *It is what they are.*

Tournier concludes, "All I can hope for when my time for action is over, is that I may yet go further in the riches of this knowledge."

The apostle Paul said that he would rather be with the Lord than be in the body, which included ministry work, hard work, more misunderstanding and challenges to his authority, more disappointments. But doing it all *with* God made it worthwhile. Yet he longed to be in God's presence. Paul's attitude at the close of his life is astonishing. He is alone, wondering if Timothy is going to desert him. But Paul acts as if he has won a gold medal at the Olympics and is about to receive it with the cheers of everyone in the universe (see 2 Tim 4:6-8).

Paul was confident of his reward, the full experience of life "put to rights," life as it should be, righteousness. Reflecting on these lessons has caused me to recall Dallas Willard's words that both stopped me and changed my life: "In the end Keith, what God gets from your ministry for him is *you*." I have found that when God stops us long enough to *get* us, others will stop and be caught up in what we are doing with him.

John Henry Newman had a kingdom perspective on life, saying, "Life is short. Death is certain: And the world to come is everlasting!" Newman also had a prayer concerning the end of life, which I keep on my desk. I often refer to it in the evening when fear or tiredness begins to shake the confidence that I had in the morning. Every evening I remember that the next day could be my last—and I wait and hasten.

O Lord, support us all the day long,
Until the shadows lengthen and the evening comes,
And the busy world is hushed, and the fever of life is over,
    and our work is done.
Then in Thy mercy grant us a safe lodging,
 and a holy rest, and peace at the last.
Amen.

Conclusion

Dad, Will You Ride with Me?

I had the privilege of accompanying my twenty-five-year-old son as he qualified for his golf pro status by completing the Professional Golf Association player's ability test. To become a golf pro he had to play two rounds of eighteen holes on one day and score within a certain number of strokes. He played well and passed, a feat few accomplish the first time. Most have to try again and again.

None of the other pros at the event had a partner like me, and certainly not their dads! I asked Kyle why he asked me to ride along. He said something I will never forget: "Dad, you calm me down."

Immediately my mind flashed to that day so many years before when Kyle's question—"Dad, are you home yet?"—stopped me in my tracks and called me away from preoccupation with ministry success, which was pulling me out of his life. He helped me on my way home to a different kind of life with God, my family and others—a kind of life that others want because it leads to home, to God and to each other. The whole life transformation in Christ I modeled to Kyle touched him and caused him to want my influence.

CONCLUDING WORDS OF ENCOURAGEMENT

It has been quite some time now since Kyle asked me if I was home yet. It seems like a lifetime ago. And it really was just that, another life. In coming home to my own transformation, inviting God into every aspect of my life, I lost the life I once was leading to find my real life, the one God was waiting to give me.

Regarding these life-changing moments Paul Tournier says,

> In every life are a few special moments that count for more than all the rest because they meant the taking of a stand, a self-commitment, a decisive choice. . . . They may have been slow, almost unconscious, gradually brought to fruition through extended crisis, or they may have been like the flash of lightning, a sudden burst into consciousness of a process worked through in the subconscious.

Tournier explains what his own "turn" to Jesus has meant for his life as he faces old age: "Ever since, Jesus Christ has become my unseen companion of every day, the witness of all my successes and all my failure. . . . All I can hope, when my time for action will be over, is that I may yet go further in the riches of this knowledge."

Through most of the writing of this book, I was executive pastor of Church of the Open Door. However, now I am entering a new ministry of equipping pastors who want to pursue whole life transformation for themselves and their congregations, becoming the change they are praying for God to bring to their churches, the change their church needs.

In a strange twist to the story of the prodigal son, God called me through Kyle to make a decisive choice for my life, from being lost in a far country of ministry distraction to life with him and others. What a surprise it was to find the Father calling me home, through the words of a child, to a banquet of family and friends. It's a journey in which we ride along with the triune God. Enjoying his calming company in the midst of life's trials and tests, we know the results are going to be better than we can imagine, as we wait and hasten for his kingdom to fully come.

Acknowledgments

Thanks to all those named below who played some part in my life and so, this work and its birth, progress and completion. My formation family—to Cheri, for tolerating the books scattered everywhere around the house and for your faithful love every day and patient support of me during this and all seasons of life; to son, Kyle, daughter and son-in-law, Cara and Mike Perszyck, for putting up with my obsession with this project, and keeping me centered.

My parents, Dr. Kenneth and Carol Meyer, for your faithful love, leading me to Jesus, his saving grace, for your faithful service to the Crystal and Rockford Evangelical Free churches, and for making a "p.k.'s" home full of fun, for an education at both Wheaton College and your legacy, Trinity International University.

My extended family and in-laws, for your encouragement and, as promised, a nod to my nephew Nathan—"When you going to write that book, Uncle Keith?"

Dr. Will Larson, psychiatrist, for your healing eyes, ears and life-saving words for me, my marriage, my family and ministry, and now my writing.

Don Cousins, for your years of listening and praying with me, your story and vulnerability and expertise, and for modeling the kind of life that churches need—full of the fruit of the Spirit.

Dallas Willard, for your kingdom example and teaching, and for your gentle but persistent admonition, "you should really write down these things that God is teaching you."

Father Jim Deegan, O.M.I., for your directing me in the Ignatian version of the school of PIU (Purgation, Illumination, Union), and the Kings House Retreat Center for all the years of serving my church staff.

Rev. John Ackerman, for helping me and our my church staff to "stop, look and listen" and notice "what God is doing now."

Father Anthony Coniaris and Paul Karos of St. Mary's Greek Orthodox Church, for modeling to me "Askesis for Theosis by Penthos and Nepsis" (Training for "God"-liness by Repentance and Watchfulness) . . . what this book is hopefully about.

Janet Hagberg, for guiding me on God's "unsafe way in the dark," and the monthly reminder to keep "drinking from water deep down in the well, where its best."

Sr. Pastor David and Bonnie Johnson, the staff and people of Church of the Open Door where I served as executive pastor for seventeen years, as well as Maple Grove, Harper and Fox Lake Evangelical Free Churches where I served as senior pastor, for the schools of formation and service opportunities they provided for me.

Howard and Janice Baker, Mike and Kate Glerup, Keith Matthews, Joel Warne, for your friendship during both difficult and delightful times, and for your partnership.

Bishop Sandy Greene and his wife, Gigi, my priest, Christian Ruch and his wife, Molly, and Church of the Cross (Hopkins, Minnesota), for providing my family and me a new church home, and to the Anglican Mission in the Americas (AMiA) and its trinity of the Scriptures, the Sacred and the Spirit.

Ken Nelson, Rockford Guilford High School English Teacher, for teaching me how to journal—to write from my heart—and for introducing me to people like C. S. Lewis!

Alan and Marilyn Youel, for first asking me to write the story "Are you Home Yet?" for the *Thin Places* newsletter (Westminster Presbyterian Church, Minneapolis, MN), and for your faithful prayers.

Bob Howey, for your generous support, the Theological and Cultural Thinkers Group, and Alan Andrews and Bill Thrall for asking me to write a chapter for *The Kingdom Life: A Practical Theology of Discipleship and Spiritual Formation,* writing that led to this IVP book, and also NavPress and Don Simpson for permission to use it.

Denver Seminary's Doctor of Ministry director, Dr. David Osborn, and my students over the years, for the opportunity to learn and teach this material with you.

My IVP Formatio editor, Cindy Bunch, who kept after me as a busy executive pastor to get "something" to her, and was so supportive and helpful to a timid writer's first shot at a book. And many thanks to the whole IVP team, what a privilege to work with you all.

Notes

Introduction

pp. 17-18   a "pose or by a constant and grinding effort": Dallas Willard, *Spirit of the Disciplines* (San Francisco: Harper & Row, 1988), p. 14.

Chapter 1: The Transformation Gap

p. 22   "It is not a want of faith in Christ": Henry Ward Beecher, quote in Debby Applegate, *The Most Famous Man in America* (New York: Doubleday, 2006), p. 256.

p. 23   "Sanctification gap": Richard Lovelace, *Dynamics of Spiritual Life* (Downers Grove, Ill.: InterVarsity Press, 1979), pp. 229-37.

p. 33   Grace, for both authors: Dallas Willard, *The Divine Conspiracy* (San Francisco: Harper SanFrancisco, 1998), p. 403, nn. 4, 5. In conversation with Dallas I learned that Mike Yaconelli had changed his view and believed that more change was possible.

p. 35   Coffee shop story: Philip Yancey, *What's So Amazing About Grace?* (Grand Rapids: Zondervan, 1997), pp. 179-80.

p. 37   "Grace is, as Frederick Buechner says, 'life itself'": Frederick Buechner, *Now and Then* (San Francisco: Harper & Row, 1983), p. 108.

p. 40   "Fight like a soldier and if you sometimes collapse": Thomas à Kempis, *The Imitation of Christ*, trans. Joseph N. Tylenda (New York: Random House, 1998), pp. 84, 122. For a contemporary translation and study guide for journaling *Imitation to Christ,* I recommend *Imitation of Christ: A Spiritual Commentary and Reader's Guide* by Dennis J. Billy (Notre Dame, Ind.: Ave Maria Press, 2005). This is the version my students use.

Chapter 2: The Double Life

p. 44   "When successful, spiritual formation . . . unites the divided heart and life": Dallas Willard, *Renovation of the Heart* (Colorado Springs: NavPress, 2002), p. 30.

p. 47 Bill Hybels tells of his pain: Greg Hawkins, Cally Parkinson and Eric Arnson, *Reveal: Where Are You?* (Barrington, Ill.: Willow Creek Resources, 2007), p. 4.

pp. 49-50 "One of the most persistent mistakes": Walter Rauschenbusch, *Christianity and the Social Crisis in the 21st Century*, ed. Paul B. Raushenbush (New York: HarperOne, 2007), p. 283.

p. 51 "It is hard for most current Evangelicals": Tony Campolo, "A Response by an Evangelical," *Christianity and the Social Crisis in the 21st Century*, ed. Paul B. Raushenbush (New York: HarperOne, 2007), p. 77.

p. 53 "I know you want to hear about the learning organization": Peter Senge, Leadership Network National Conference, "Exploring Off the Map," Denver, May 2000.

Chapter 3: What Ministry Masks

p. 64 "combine the dry wood of the average consumer Christian": Kent Carlson, personal conversation (September 5, 2004).

pp. 64-65 "These pastors, counselors, and others": Sandra Wilson, *Counseling Adult Children of Alcoholics* (Dallas: Word, 1989), p. 268.

p. 65 transference happens a lot in churches and religious organizations: Valerie McIntyre, *Sheep in Wolves' Clothing* (Grand Rapids: Baker, 1996), pp. 77-111.

p. 65 transference occurs between employees and supervisors: Scott Peck, "Who's There: Roles and Transference," *A World Waiting to Be Born* (New York: Bantam Books, 1993), pp. 195-218.

p. 70 Alcoholics Anonymous as the greatest event: Scott Peck, *The Road Less Traveled*, quote in Leonard I. Sweet, *Strong in the Broken Places* (Akron, Ohio: University of Akron Press, 1995), p. xi.

p. 71 ancients teachings submitted to scientific testing: Diogenes Allen, *Lymning the Psyche* (Grand Rapids: Eerdmans, 1997), pp. 297-316.

p. 71 Sigmund Freud and Carl Jung: I believe that both Freud and Jung provide some helpful insights for understanding ourselves as beings with desires and personalities that make up character, but their solutions are materialist (Freud) or even influenced by the occult (Jung). See Jeffrey Satinover, *The Empty Self* (Westport, Conn.: Hamewith Books, 1996).

p. 71 These dangerous ideas came: Leanne Payne, *Heaven's Calling*

(Grand Rapids: Baker, 2008), pp. 241-42.

p. 72 In *The Broken Image:* Leanne Payne, *The Broken Image* (Grand Rapids: Baker, 1981).

p. 74 those with addictions or psychological problems: Thomas Green, *Weeds Among the Wheat* (Notre Dame, Ind.: Ave Maria Press, 1984), pp. 100-102.

Chapter 4: Church as Business

p. 78 "organizational extension and survival": Darrell L. Guder, ed., *Missional Church* (Grand Rapids: Eerdmans, 1998), pp. 5, 217.

p. 82 Eugene Peterson tells of his decision to stay in one church: Eugene Peterson, *Under the Unpredictable Plant* (Grand Rapids: Eerdmans, 1992), p. 18

pp. 82-83 "the norm for pastoral work": Ibid., p. 29.

p. 87 "the success heresy": Don Cousins, *LeaderShift* (Colorado Springs: Cook, 2008), pp. 74-75.

p. 88 "failing to act according to their size": Lyle Schaller, "The Consequences of Consumerism," *The Very Large Church* (Nashville: Abingdon, 2000), pp. 76-104.

p. 89 people who start churches trade away meaningful relationships: David E. Fitch, *The Great Giveaway: Reclaiming the Mission of the Church from Big Business, Parachurch Organizations, Psychotherapy, Consumer Capitalism and Other Modern Maladies* (Grand Rapids: Baker, 2005), pp. 27-33. I do not agree with Fitch's views on the inability of larger churches to be tranformational. See also Keith Meyer, "The Megachurch and the Monastery," *Leadership Journal* (Winter 2009): 40-44. This article proposes ways larger churches can be centered on transformation but does ask the question, is megachurch discipleship an oxymoron? Large churches do not necessarily have to sacrifice formation for size, but size certainly presents some very difficult challenges to formation ministry, and often the retooling will risk the dilemmas spelled out in Schaller's chapter "The Consequences of Consumerism" in *The Very Large Church.*

p. 89 "few pastors": George Barna, *Growing True Disciples* (Colorado Springs: Waterbrook, 2001), pp. 95-96.

p. 93 by 2025 only 30 percent: George Barna, *Revolution* (Wheaton, Ill.: Tyndale House, 2005), pp. 48-49.

p. 93 profile of the "churchless faithful": Alan Jamieson, *Churchless Faith* (London: SPCK, 2002), p. 15.

pp. 93-94   American church attendance is in actual decline: David Olsen, *The American Church in Crisis* (Grand Rapids: Zondervan, 2008), pp. 36-38.

p. 94   "Moody, save all you can": George M. Marsden, "The Era of Crisis: From Christendom to Pluralism," in *Eerdmans' Handbook to Christianity in America*, ed. Mark Noll et al. (Grand Rapids: Eerdmans, 1983), pp. 294-95.

p. 95   Charles Reich's Consciousness I and II: Richard Lovelace, *Dynamics of Spiritual Life* (Downers Grove, Ill.: InterVarsity Press, 1979), pp. 377-78.

Chapter 5: Formation by Family and Friends

p. 99   missing the importance of ordinary relationships: Susan S. Phillips, *Candlelight: Illuminating the Art of Spiritual Direction* (New York: Morehouse, 2008), p. 2.

p. 100   "The real love of man must depend on practice": John Henry Newman, *Selected Sermons, Prayers, and Devotions by John Henry Newman*, ed. John F. Thornton and Susan B. Varenne (New York: Random House, 1999), p. 76.

p. 105   false selves and the true self: Judith Hougen, *Transformed into Fire: Discovering Your True Identity as God's Beloved* (Grand Rapids: Kregel, 2002), pp. 87-104. See also "Stopping Lessons: Ministry from a Life of Sabbatical Rest," *Journal of Spiritual Formation and Soul Care* 1, no. 2 (2008): 217-31

p. 108   "the gift to be sensitive, present and supportive to the spiritual journey of another": Daniel F. Stramara, pamphlet 24, *What Is Spiritual Direction?* (Pecos, N.M.: Dove Publications).

p. 108   spiritual direction as "holy listening": Margaret Guenther, *Holy Listening* (Boston: Cowley, 1992), p. 1.

p. 108   "the problem with the term spiritual direction": Eugene Peterson, "The Extraordinary Ordinary," *Heart and Mind* 5, no. 3 (1991): 5, italic in original.

pp. 110-11   "In the best of all possible worlds": Ibid., p. 6.

p. 112   "The man who keeps secret his most painful memories": Paul Tournier, *The Meaning of Persons* (New York: Harper & Row, 1957), pp. 158-59.

p. 112   "A Great Old Lover": As I mentioned in chapter one, C. S. Lewis describes the challenge every marriage faces to move from a "young love" to a "great old love" in his advice to Sheldon Vanauken in *A Severe Mercy*.

p. 115   MacDonald selections from *Donal Grant* and *Salted with Fire*:
            Rolland Hein, *The World of George MacDonald: Selections from
            His Works of Fiction* (Wheaton, Ill.: Harold Shaw, 1978), p. 13.

p. 116   "the reward of parents who have tried to be good": Ibid., p. 60.

p. 117   "Your enjoyment of the world is never right": Thomas Traherne,
            Centuries of Meditations (New York: Cosimo Classics, 2007),
            pp. 19, 25.

p. 118   "Let Me So Eye Thee": Ibid., p. 63.

Chapter 6: Church as a Catching Force

p. 129   "being the cooperative friends of Jesus": Todd D. Hunter, *Chris-
            tianity Beyond Belief: Following Jesus for the Sake of Others*
            (Downers Grove, Ill.: InterVarsity Press, 2009), pp. 28, 75-91.

p. 135   "While the charge was to make disciples of Jesus and *not* of the
            disciples": Dallas Willard, "Discipleship," in *The Oxford Hand-
            book of Evangelical Theology,* ed. Gerald R. McDermott (Ox-
            ford: Oxford University Press, forthcoming). This
            much-anticipated work includes articles by Mark Noll, Alister
            McGrath, Kevin VanHoozer, Scot McKnight, Gordon T. Smith,
            Simon Chan and others.

Chapter 7: Training for a Trust That Obeys

p. 151   "For most of Western history, the basic claims of the Christian
            tradition": Dallas Willard, *Knowing Christ Today: Why We Can
            Trust Spiritual Knowledge* (New York: HarperOne, 2009), p. 8.

p. 151   "It is now widely thought": Ibid., p. 49.

p. 152   "The difference between belief and knowledge": Ibid., p. 15.

p. 157   "I was kicked, and flogged, and pinched": Mary Prince, "The
            History of Mary Prince, a West Indian Slave," p. 7, available at
            <http://docsouth.unc.edu/neh/prince/prince.html>.

p. 158   "When I found out that I was a great sinner": Ibid., p. 17.

p. 159   "Grant us, even us, O Lord": Augustine, *Ancient Christian De-
            votional*, ed. Thomas Oden and Cindy Crosby (Downers Grove,
            Ill.: InterVarsity Press, 2007), p. 71.

Chapter 8: Ruling in Kingdom Life

p. 174   the average American watched TV for 151 hours a month: The
            Nielson Three Screen Report <www.cnn.com/2009/showbiz/
            tv/02/24/us.video.nielson>.

p. 180   "[Jesus] did not form an army": D. Elton Trueblood, *Alternative to Futility* (San Francisco: Harper & Row, 1948), p. 29.

p. 181   "the Fellowship": Thomas Kelly, *A Testament of Devotion* (New York: HarperCollins, 1992), pp. 26-34, 51-61.

pp. 182-83   "May the Mind of Christ My Savior": Kate B. Wilkinson (1925).

Chapter 9: Leaving the Results to God

p. 187   "leave the results to God" and "don't sweat it": Dallas Willard, spoken various times when I have heard him teach and in conversations.

pp. 190-91   Maximillian Kolbe's story: Robert Ellsberg, *All Saints* (New York: Crossroad, 1997), p. 35.

p. 192   "like the Christian's sanctification, Christian community is a gift of God": Dietrich Bonhoeffer, *Life Together* (San Francisco: Harper & Row, 1954), p. 30.

p. 195   "empty-handed," "unattached love" and "hopeless hope": Gerald May, *The Dark Night of the Soul* (New York: HarperCollins, 2004), p. 194.

p. 195   Johann and Christoph Blumhardt: Vernard Elder, ed., *Thy Kingdom Come: A Blumhardt Reader* (Grand Rapids: Eerdmans, 1980), pp. xvii-xx. The Blumhardts are relatively unknown in America, but their writings are being compiled by Bethel University professor Christian Collins Winn and Plough editor Charles Moore. For more information, contact Charles Moore at www.plough.com or Christian Collins Winn at ctcollin@bethel.edu.

p. 196   "There must be a new reality which is of the truth": Johann Blumhardt, in ibid., p. 3.

p. 197   "it was more important to be cleansed than healed": Christoph Blumhardt, in ibid., p. xix.

pp. 197-98   "It helps, now and then, to step back and take a long view": Oscar Romero prayer, printed in a reprint edition of Christoph Blumhardt's *Action in Waiting* (Rifton, N.Y.: Plough, 1998), pp. xxx-xxxi. The prayer was actually written by Ken Uhtener; see <http://bogners.typepad.com/church/2004/03/the_prayer_of_o.html>.

pp. 199-200 "People are often unreasonable, illogical and self-centered": Written on the wall of Mother Teresa's home for children in Calcutta, her version of *The Paradoxical Commandments* by Dr. Kent M. Keith, a 1968 booklet for student leaders.

p. 200   "The die is cast": Paul Tournier, *The Seasons of Life* (Atlanta: John Knox Press, 1966), pp. 55, 61, italic in original.

p. 201   "Life is short. Death is certain": John Henry Newman, *Selected Sermons, Prayers and Devotions,* ed. John F. Thornton and Susan B. Varenne (New York: Vintage Spiritual Classics, 1999), p. xxix.

p. 201   "O Lord, support us all the day long": Paraphrase from the Book of Common Prayer, quoted by Newman in ibid., p. 385.

Conclusion

p. 204   "In every life are a few special moments": Paul Tournier, *The Seasons of Life* (Atlanta: John Knox Press, 1966), p. 58.

p. 204   "Ever since, Jesus Christ has become my unseen companion": Ibid., p. 61.

About the Author

Take Your Next Step into Becoming the Change

Keith invites you to visit and contact him at his website, **www.keithmeyer.org**.

Learn about the various ways he can resource your life and ministry through speaking, teaching, training seminars, personal coaching and organizational consulting (online, Skype or onsite visits).

He also leads retreats for pastors and their spouses, church staff teams, marketplace leaders and students, and helps in the planning and creation of your own yearly cycles of corporate and individual retreat rhythms.

Create your own life-changing "rule of life" with Keith's coaching and by becoming a practicing member of The Order of the Renovated Heart. This is a cyber-blogging community of apprentices to Jesus sharing their experiences by intentionally envisioning and training to become individual and corporate examples for others—a catching force for God's kingdom.

You can also support the work of training pastors and leaders through contributing to the BTC Foundation.

Becoming The Change Ministries (Nonprofit)
The BTC Foundation
Keith Meyer Consulting, LLC

"Be the Change That the World Is Waiting to See"

*f*ormatio
TRADITION. EXPERIENCE.
TRANSFORMATION.

Formatio books from InterVarsity Press follow the rich tradition of the church in the journey of spiritual formation. These books are not merely about being informed, but about being transformed by Christ and conformed to his image. Formatio stands in InterVarsity Press's evangelical publishing tradition by integrating God's Word with spiritual practice and by prompting readers to move from inward change to outward witness. InterVarsity Press uses the chambered nautilus for Formatio, a symbol of spiritual formation because of its continual spiral journey outward as it moves from its center. We believe that each of us is made with a deep desire to be in God's presence. Formatio books help us to fulfill our deepest desires and to become our true selves in light of God's grace.